THE CHURCH:
PURPOSE, PROFILE, PRIORITIES

BIBLE STUDY GUIDE

From the Bible-teaching ministry of

Charles R. Swindoll

Charles R. Swindoll is a graduate of Dallas Theological Seminary and has served in pastorates for more than twenty-five years, including churches in Texas, New England, and California. Since 1971 he has served as senior pastor of the First Evangelical Free Church of Fullerton, California. Chuck's radio program, "Insight for Living," began in 1979. In addition to his church and radio ministries, Chuck enjoys writing. He has authored numerous books and booklets on a variety of subjects.

Based on the outlines of Chuck's sermons, the study guide text is coauthored by Ken Gire, a graduate of Texas Christian University and Dallas Theological Seminary. The Living Insights are written by Bill Butterworth, a graduate of Florida Bible College, Dallas Theological Seminary, and Florida Atlantic University. Ken Gire is presently the director of educational products at Insight for Living, and Bill Butterworth is currently a staff writer in the Educational Products Department.

Editor in Chief:	Cynthia Swindoll
Coauthor of Text:	Ken Gire
Author of Living Insights:	Bill Butterworth
Assistant Editor:	Karene Wells
Copy Manager:	Jac La Tour
Senior Copy Editor:	Jane Gillis
Copy Editor:	Kevin Moritz
Director, Communications Division:	Carla Beck
Project Manager:	Nina Paris
Project Supervisor:	Cassandra Clark
Designer:	Jenkins & Jenkins
Production Artists:	Steve Cox and Diana Vasquez
Typographer:	Bob Haskins
Cover Photographer:	Rudi Weislein
Print Production Manager:	Deedee Snyder
Printer:	Frye and Smith

ISBN 0-8499-8401-7

Ordering Information

An album that contains ten messages on five cassettes and corresponds to this study guide may be purchased through the Sales Department of Insight for Living, Post Office Box 4444, Fullerton, California 92634. For ordering information and a current catalog, please write our office or call 1-800-772-8888.

Canadian residents may obtain a catalog and ordering information through Insight for Living Ministries, Post Office Box 2510, Vancouver, British Columbia, Canada V6B 3W7, 1-800-663-7639. Australian residents should direct their correspondence to Insight for Living Ministries, General Post Office Box 2823 EE, Melbourne, Victoria 3001. Other overseas residents should direct their correspondence to our Fullerton office.

If you wish to order by Visa or MasterCard, you are welcome to use our toll-free number, 1-800-772-8888, Monday through Friday, between the hours of 8:30 A.M. and 4:00 P.M., Pacific time. This number may be used anywhere in the United States. Orders from Canada can be made by calling 1-800-663-7639.

Table of Contents

*This message was not a part of the original series but is compatible with it.

The Church: Purpose, Profile, Priorities

Haven't you wondered about the underlying purpose of the church these days? Her goals and priorities? Her role?

Thanks to the confusion brought on by religious charlatans and gurus, many Christians are no longer sure of the local church's place in today's society. Some doubt her significance and question their own responsibility to remain loyal and faithful. A mild indifference is spreading like a cancer. "Who cares?" accompanied by a shrug, is the reaction of many who once believed strongly in the church's calling. It is a fact that more people than ever now doubt her integrity.

This brief yet potent study addresses issues that matter. I bring these messages to you as a pastor, a caring shepherd . . . not as a "media minister." As you will be able to detect, I feel deeply about the principles we shall uncover from God's Word.

So, have your Bible ready. Keep your heart right. Open your mind. Pray. This series could be the turning point for some who have begun to wander from the church. Who knows? Even you *may discover an area or two that needs some attention.*

Chuck Swindoll

Chuck Swindoll

Putting Truth into Action

Knowledge apart from application falls short of God's desire for His children. Knowledge must result in change and growth. Consequently, we have constructed this Bible study guide with these purposes in mind: (1) to stimulate discovery, (2) to increase understanding, and (3) to encourage application.

At the end of each lesson is a section called ***Living Insights.*** *There you'll be given assistance in further Bible study, and you'll be encouraged to contemplate and apply the things you've learned. This is the place where the lesson is fitted with shoe leather for your walk through the varied experiences of life.*

It's our hope that you'll discover numerous ways to use this tool. Some useful avenues we suggest are personal meditation, joint discovery, and discussion with your spouse, family, work associates, friends, or neighbors. The study guide is also practical for Sunday school classes, Bible study groups, and, of course, as a study aid for the "Insight for Living" radio broadcast.

In order to derive the greatest benefit from this process, we suggest that you record your responses to the lessons in the space which has been provided for you. In view of the kinds of questions asked, your study guide may become a journal filled with your many discoveries and commitments. We anticipate that you will find yourself returning to it periodically for review and encouragement.

Ken Gire

Ken Gire
Coauthor of Text

Bill Butterworth

Bill Butterworth
Author of Living Insights

THE CHURCH:
PURPOSE, PROFILE, PRIORITIES

The Taproot Purpose of Our Existence

Selected Scripture

Socrates was wise, it is said, not because he knew the right answers, but because he knew how to ask the right questions.

And of all questions, none delves to the depths of an issue faster than *why.*

The Old Testament is replete with penetrating *whys.* God asked Cain: "Why are you angry?" The Lord asked Abraham: "Why did Sarah laugh?" Moses asked: "Why is the bush not burned up?" Nathan asked David: "Why have you despised the Word of the Lord?" Job asked: "Why did I not die at birth?"

Turning to the New Testament, *why* seems to be Jesus' favorite question. "Why are you anxious?... Why do you look at the speck in your brother's eye?... Why do you call Me, 'Lord, Lord,' and do not do what I say?... Why do you not believe Me?... Why have You forsaken Me?"

Why has a way of tearing through the superficial husk of a matter and shucking right down to the cob. The *why* we are asking today is no exception: "Why does the church exist?" The question is one of purpose. When all the extras are set aside, when we dig right down to the taproot reason for our being on earth at this time, what do we find?

The answer to that question should radically affect the way we think and live.

I. The Primary Issue

Like Socrates, we want to learn to ask the right questions. Because, like picks and shovels, good questions are the best way to uncover what's not so obvious on the surface.

A. Question: "Why are we in existence as a local church?"

The array of possible answers might be: to present the gospel to the lost... to bring hope to the hurting... to provide a place of worship and instruction... to equip saints for the work of ministry . . . to comfort the grieving . . . to feed the hungry . . . to help the needy. While all of these are certainly worthwhile reasons and a part of the greater picture, they are not the primary reason for the church's existence.

B. Answer: "To glorify the Lord our God." Turn to the tenth chapter of 1 Corinthians, verse 31, which explicitly states the reason for our existence.

> Whether, then, you eat or drink or whatever you do, do all to the glory of God.

Go back a few pages to chapter 6, and you'll see Paul reiterate our purpose.

> Or do you not know that your body is a temple of the Holy Spirit who is in you, whom you have from God, and that you are not your own? For you have been bought with a price: therefore glorify God in your body. (vv. 19–20)

Back in the book of Romans, Paul articulates the same purpose for the church.

> Now may the God who gives perseverance and encouragement grant you to be of the same mind with one another according to Christ Jesus; that with one accord you may with one voice glorify the God and Father of our Lord Jesus Christ. (15:5–6)

Even though the New Testament throbs with the consuming purpose to glorify God, our twentieth-century pulse grows faint on this point. Our hearts beat more in rhythm with corporate America than with the early church, more with Madison Avenue than with the manuscripts of the New Testament. We think our goal is growth. After all, isn't bigger better? Often our goal is to make an impression, to look good, to have stirring music and scintillating sermons. But why? Why do we preach? Why do we sing? Why do we serve? Only one answer is acceptable, and that is to glorify God. Second Thessalonians 1:11–12 supports this answer.

> To this end also we pray for you always that our God may count you worthy of your calling, and fulfill every desire for goodness and the work of faith with power; in order that the name of our Lord Jesus may be glorified in you, and you in Him, according to the grace of our God and the Lord Jesus Christ.

Note the reciprocal action in these verses. As you glorify God, you will be glorified in Him. And when others observe your life, they will want to glorify Him, too, as Matthew 5:16 affirms.

> "Let your light shine before men in such a way that they may see your good works, and glorify your Father who is in heaven."[1]

It is, then, abundantly clear that the taproot purpose of our existence is just what the Westminster *Shorter Catechism* suggests: to glorify God, and to enjoy Him forever.

II. An Analysis of the Answer

Let's take that nugget of truth about glorifying God and run a more exacting assay on it.

A. What does it mean?

A. What does it mean? Scripture uses *glory* in a variety of ways, but three meanings are most common.

1. **A bright, shining light.** The Shekinah[2] glory, spoken of in Exodus 40:34, is a good example of this.

   > Then the cloud covered the tent of meeting, and the glory of the Lord filled the tabernacle.

   God led the Israelites through the wilderness with a pillar of cloud by day and of fire by night. But when the tabernacle was finished and His presence rested in the Holy of Holies, He took the form of a brilliant, blinding light.

2. **A unique representation or distinctive appearance.** Turning to 1 Corinthians 15:39–41, we find the word *glory* used of celestial bodies.

   > All flesh is not the same flesh, but there is one flesh of men, and another flesh of beasts, and another flesh of birds, and another of fish. There are also heavenly bodies and earthly bodies, but the glory of the heavenly is one, and the glory of the earthly is another. There is one glory of the sun, and another glory of the moon, and another glory of the stars; for star differs from star in glory.

   Glory, in this passage, refers to the unique characteristics of every created thing.

3. **To magnify or elevate, shedding radiance or splendor on another.** What does it mean to glorify God? It means to magnify and elevate the Lord God as we diminish and deny ourselves. This is best illustrated by John the Baptizer, who

1. See also Matthew 9:1–8 and 1 Peter 2:11–12, 4:11–16.

2. *Shekinah* means literally "dwelling of God." It denotes the visible presence of God and is alluded to in Isaiah 60:2 as "His glory" and in Romans 9:4 as "the glory." Moses refers to this as the "cloud" in Exodus 14:19 (see also Exod. 13:21; 14:20, 24). See "Shekinah," *The New Compact Bible Dictionary,* ed. T. Alton Bryant (Grand Rapids, Mich.: Zondervan Publishing House, 1967), p. 544.

said: "He must increase, but I must decrease" (John 3:30). John was the voice (1:23); Jesus was the Word (vv. 1, 14). John was only a man; Jesus was Messiah. John did not even consider himself worthy to untie the thong of the Savior's sandal (v. 27; see also vv. 29–30). Glorifying God means being occupied with and committed to God's ways rather than preoccupied with and determined to accomplish our own ways. So often these two desires conflict, as Isaiah 55 notes.

> "Why do you spend money for what is not bread,
> And your wages for what does not satisfy?
> Listen carefully to Me, and eat what is good,
> And delight yourself in abundance. . . .
> For My thoughts are not your thoughts,
> Neither are your ways My ways," declares the Lord.
> "For as the heavens are higher than the earth,
> So are My ways higher than your ways,
> And My thoughts than your thoughts."
> (vv. 2, 8–9)

In Psalm 145, David shows what it means to give glory to God.

> I will extol Thee, my God, O King;
> And I will bless Thy name forever and ever.
> Every day I will bless Thee,
> And I will praise Thy name forever and ever.
> (vv. 1–2)

Have you ever tried that? Ever exalted the Lord that explicitly and that enthusiastically? Of course, it's easy to praise the Lord when you have the wind at your back and you're sailing smoothly along. But what about the times when the wind is whipping you in the face? Can you give glory to Him then? Take a look at another time in David's life, when the bottom dropped out and he had nowhere to look but up. Same man. Same God. Same spirit of praise.

> Incline Thine ear, O Lord, and answer me;
> For I am afflicted and needy.
> Do preserve my soul, for I am a godly man;
> O Thou my God, save Thy servant who trusts in Thee. . . .
> In the day of my trouble I shall call upon Thee,
> For Thou wilt answer me. (86:1–2, 7)

Praise from the Pit

In the day of his trouble, David called upon the Lord. In the day of your trouble, whom do you call upon?

In the day of financial trouble, do you try to "master the possibilities" with your charge cards—or do you call upon the Master? In the day of trouble in finding God's will, do you seek out the counsel of man—or do you seek out the one whose name is Wonderful, Counselor, Prince of Peace?

Maybe reviewing a few more verses from David's song will encourage you to sing praises to God when times look bleak, instead of singing the blues.

> There is no one like Thee among the gods,
> O Lord;
> Nor are there any works like Thine....
> For Thou art great and doest wondrous
> deeds;
> Thou alone art God.
> Teach me Thy way, O Lord;
> I will walk in Thy truth;
> Unite my heart to fear Thy name.
> I will give thanks to Thee, O Lord my God,
> with all my heart,
> And will glorify Thy name forever.
> (Ps. 86:8, 10–12)

B. Where does it apply? Getting down to everyday life, here are some "whens," some "ins," and some "ifs" of glorifying God in all facets of our lives.

1. **When.** When you are unsure, you glorify Him by seeking and waiting. When you need to make a decision, you glorify Him by leaning on His guidance. When affliction and suffering assault you, His glory is to be sought rather than a way out. When you're pursuing an education, His glory is the paramount issue, even down to the very selection of courses. When you find it necessary to relinquish a dream and walk away, willingly surrender it for the sake of His glory. Then, and only then, can you be assured that the highest good has been served.
2. **In.** In your public or private life, your motivation should be His glory, not your own. In relationships, His glory should be central. In your home and in your work, His glory should be the prime factor in every decision. In your studies, His

glory should be at stake, not yours. In fame and fortune, the spotlight should be on Him. And even when the spotlight fades and things look bleak, the focus should remain on God, not on yourself, and not on your circumstances.

3. **If.** If a person you love stays or leaves, God should get the glory. If a cause you support wins or loses, God should get the glory. If the plans you arrange succeed or fail or must be altered, God should get the glory.

III. Some Suggestions for Making It Happen

Now let's refine this truth about God's glory so that you can make use of it in your own life.

A. Three thoughts. Here are some suggestions for how you can take God's glory out of the realm of the theoretical and into the realm of the practical.

1. **Cultivate the habit of including the Lord in every segment of your life.** It may help to write down this question: Is God getting the glory? Put that reminder on the dashboard of your car, on your desk, on your bathroom mirror, on your refrigerator door, or in other places you frequent.
2. **Refuse to expect or accept any of the glory that ought to be God's.** Like a sponge, the flesh will soak up all the glory if given the opportunity. Everything we do can be done either in the flesh or in the Spirit—and that includes what should be done for God. *Especially* what should be done for God.
3. **Maintain a priority relationship with Him that's more important than any other on earth.** Some of you are closer to your children, your spouse, or your friends than you are to God. In Matthew 10:37–38, Jesus underscores the importance of His being number one in your life.

> "He who loves father or mother more than Me is not worthy of Me; and he who loves son or daughter more than Me is not worthy of Me. And he who does not take his cross and follow after Me is not worthy of Me."[3]

B. Three actions. To put shoe leather on the three previous thoughts, here are three corresponding actions.

1. **To help cultivate the habit of including the Lord in every segment of your life, meet with Him often and meet with Him alone.** In this fast-paced life, we often squeeze in time with the Lord on the run. But God refuses

3. See the parallel passage in Luke 14:26 where Jesus uses the strong word *hate* to draw a dramatic contrast. The point Jesus is making is that any other relationship, no matter how close, should pale in comparison to our love for Him—so much so, that when placed side by side, the contrast would be as sharp as between love and hate.

to be anyone's fast food. If we want a relationship with Him that permeates every area of our lives, we must carve out the time and cultivate that relationship. It may be early in the morning or late at night. It may be ten uninterrupted minutes or two hours. But it must be often. And it must be undistracted time alone with Him.

2. **To help not to expect or accept any of the glory, openly admit your struggle with pride.** Tell your family. Tell a support group to which you're accountable. Just like recovering alcoholics who publicly admit their problem, so you must publicly admit your pride as the first step in overcoming it.
3. **To help maintain that priority relationship with Him, filter everything through this question: Will this bring glory to God, or to me?** The answer to that searching question can be easily faked. You can pretend to give glory to God when all the while you're piously soaking it up like a sponge. Don't fake humility. The Pharisees tried it in Jesus' day, and He saw right through them. And, by the way, so did most everyone else.

A Concluding Thought

Socrates once said:

> Bad men live that they may eat and drink, whereas good men eat and drink that they may live.[4]

A wiser man, Solomon, gave us a richer perspective:

> There is nothing better for a man than to eat and drink and tell himself that his labor is good. This also I have seen, that it is from the hand of God. For who can eat and who can have enjoyment without Him? (Eccles. 2:24–25)

But in the New Testament, Paul takes that thought to still a higher plane:

> Whether, then, you eat or drink or whatever you do, do all to the glory of God. (1 Cor. 10:31)

And if we are wise, we, too, will have that as our primary motivation in life.

4. *Bartlett's Familiar Quotations,* 14th ed., rev. and enl., ed. Emery Morison Beck (Boston, Mass.: Little, Brown and Co., 1968), p. 87.

Living Insights

Study One

Socrates was wise, not because he knew the right answers, but because he knew how to ask the right questions. Let's take a page from his notebook and ask some questions about the series before us.

- Take this opportunity to briefly peruse the next nine lesson outlines in this study guide. Use the following space to record questions that come to your mind as you look over the topics. Then watch God answer your questions as the lessons unfold in the coming days.

The Church: Purpose, Profile, Priorities

Living Insights

Study Two

Let's continue our preview of this series. Turning our attention away from questions, let's look for areas of personal application.

- Go back over all ten lessons this time and write down any truths that catch your eye which you might want to apply to your life.

The Church: Purpose, Profile, Priorities

The WIFE Every Church Should Marry

Acts 2:41–47

Ministry is a little like mercury—it's hard to get a grip on it. And even if you do, it's easy to mishandle it and hurt people. Because ministry, like mercury, can be dangerous.

For example, if a thermometer broke in your mouth and you ingested the mercury in it, the result could be mercury poisoning. The absorbed mercury is concentrated in the kidneys where it poisons the blood-filtering structures, affecting you not only physically but psychologically as well.

In the early 1950s, there was an outbreak of mercury poisoning in Minamata, Japan. The people experienced a progressive weakening of muscles, loss of vision, impaired brain functions, paralysis, and, in some cases, coma and death. The culprit was found to be industrial waste that contained mercury, which flowed from a factory into the bay, where large numbers of fish and shellfish absorbed it. As the people ate the marine life, they, too, were poisoned.

That's why at times we need to pull back from the busyness of our ministry and take a good look at what we're about, how we're doing, what we're doing, and more importantly, why.

The process of rethinking and reevaluating can be a difficult one. It's hard for us to be objective and all too easy to rationalize. Yet this willingness to be placed under scrutiny is precisely what marked David as a man after God's own heart (see Ps. 139:23–24). In our ministry, as well as our individual lives, this type of introspection is not optional; it's essential.

I. Ten Statements about Ministry

From Warren and David Wiersbe's excellent book, *Making Sense of the Ministry,* we've gleaned the following ten pieces of practical advice.[1]

A. The foundation of ministry is character. And Proverbs 4:23 tells us how to guard that character.

> Watch over your heart with all diligence,
> For from it flow the springs of life.

The streams of life flow from our inner heart. And at the heart of one who ministers must be character. Financier J. P. Morgan once commented that a man's best collateral is his character.[2]

1. Warren W. Wiersbe and David Wiersbe, *Making Sense of the Ministry* (Chicago, Ill.: Moody Press, 1983), pp. 31–46.

2. Wiersbe and Wiersbe, *Making Sense of the Ministry,* p. 34.

If you are in the ministry and your character is poor, you ought to get out of the ministry until you have corrected it.

B. **The nature of ministry is service.** The word *ministry* is from the Greek term meaning "to serve." Remember, our Lord Himself said He "did not come to be served, but to serve" (Mark 10:45a). Sadly, down through the years, we have chosen to emulate the Pharisees rather than Jesus. We have given up the role of the servant, who washes the feet of others. Instead, we seek "the place of honor at banquets, and the chief seats in the synagogues, and respectful greetings in the market places" (Matt. 23:6–7a). Jeremiah's words to his secretary, Baruch, pose a poignant question we should all ask ourselves:

> " 'But you, are you seeking great things for yourself?
> Do not seek them. . . .' " (Jer. 45:5a)

C. **The motive for ministry is love.** How prominent is love in your ministry? Pause a minute to reflect on not only what you've done but how and why you've done it . . . not only what you've said but how and why you've said it. Was the motive love?

D. **The measure of ministry is sacrifice.** John Henry Jowett's words are haunting: "Ministry that costs nothing, accomplishes nothing."[3] When was the last time you were challenged to sacrifice anything for the cause of Christ? Sacrificial ministry is merely our following in the footsteps of Christ, who went before us and led the way—a way which passed by the steep grade of Calvary's hill, where He was "to give His life a ransom for many" (Mark 10:45b). Sacrifice. That's the measure against which all ministries must stand. That's the standard set by the servant par excellence.

E. **The authority of ministry is submission.** People who command authority have no right to do so until they have learned to submit to authority. Often a person loves the idea of ministering because it's a way to exercise authority over others. But that's the wrong reason. That's pride. And nothing can destroy a ministry faster than pride.

F. **The purpose of ministry is to glorify God.** God's glory is one thing He reserves for Himself, and only Himself. He refuses to share it with anyone or anything.

> "I am the Lord, that is My name;
> I will not give My glory to another,
> Nor My praise to graven images." (Isa. 42:8)

G. **The tools of the ministry are prayer and Scripture.** Look at Acts 6:4, a verse worth frequent review.

3. Wiersbe and Wiersbe, *Making Sense of the Ministry,* p. 36.

"But we will devote ourselves to prayer, and to the ministry of the word."

Both actions are important. If we have only Bible study and no prayer, we wind up with light—but no heat. If we have only prayer and no Bible study, we have heat—but no light.

H. The privilege of ministry is growth. Growing deeper, growing closer, growing larger—these are the wonderful privileges of ministry. The book of Acts paints a beautiful mural of a church on the move.[4] Think about your ministry. How deep are you getting? How close are you growing to others? Is your faith branching out?

I. The power of ministry is the Holy Spirit. Perhaps the most often overlooked source of power in a church is the Holy Spirit. Trenchantly criticizing the organized church, A. W. Tozer once said that if the Lord removed the Holy Spirit from this world, much of what we are doing in the church would continue and nobody would even know the difference.[5] What a sad commentary on our reliance on programs instead of the dynamic power of the Spirit. Zechariah's words are as true today as the day he penned them: "Not by might nor by power, but by My Spirit" (Zech. 4:6b). The Living Bible goes on to say, "You will succeed because of my Spirit."[6]

J. The model for ministry is Jesus Christ. Many people model a ministry after a leader. They idealize and imitate a person rather than Christ. Yet no one even comes close to His example (Col. 1:16–18). David Livingstone once wisely remarked:

> He is the greatest master I have ever known. If there is anyone greater, I do not know him. Jesus Christ is the only master supremely worth serving. He is the only ideal that never loses its inspiration. He is the only friend whose friendship meets every demand. He is the only Savior who can save to the uttermost. We go forth in His name, in His power, and in His Spirit to serve Him.[7]

Imbed these ten statements about ministry in your heart, and they will keep you on target in serving God.

4. See Acts 2:47; 4:4; 5:14; 6:1, 7; 11:21; 16:5.
5. Wiersbe and Wiersbe, *Making Sense of the Ministry,* p. 44.
6. The Living Bible (Wheaton, Ill.: Tyndale House Publishers, 1971).
7. Wiersbe and Wiersbe, *Making Sense of the Ministry,* p. 46.

II. Four Major Objectives of a Church

As we turn our attention to Acts 2, we'll see four pictures of the church in its embryonic form. And from these pictures, we will be able to determine the major objectives of any local assembly that comes into existence. These objectives are cross-cultural, cross-denominational, and true in spite of the ministry's style or size. They are the specific avenues through which we are to carry out the purpose of glorifying God. Take a close look at verses 42–47, and see if you can discover the four pictures.

> And they were continually devoting themselves to the apostles' teaching and to fellowship, to the breaking of bread and to prayer. And everyone kept feeling a sense of awe; and many wonders and signs were taking place through the apostles. And all those who had believed were together, and had all things in common; and they began selling their property and possessions, and were sharing them with all, as anyone might have need. And day by day continuing with one mind in the temple, and breaking bread from house to house, they were taking their meals together with gladness and sincerity of heart, praising God, and having favor with all the people. And the Lord was adding to their number day by day those who were being saved.

To help remember the four objectives, the word *WIFE* will serve as an acronym, representing worship, instruction, fellowship, and evangelism.

A. Worship. Look again at verse 42, and you will see a body of committed, worshipful people. The Greek term, meaning "to devote," is also used in Acts 1:14 and 6:4. It connotes a steadfast, single-minded fidelity. Worship was not a half-hearted effort for the early church; it was intense. And it held a beautiful simplicity—the breaking of bread and prayer. Yet, amid those simple expressions of worship was a profound reverence, as 2:43a indicates:

> Everyone kept feeling a sense of awe.

The Greek states simply: "And came to every soul, fear." No one truly worships who doesn't possess a healthy and awesome respect for the most high, most holy God. Verse 46 suggests a unity in the worship:

> And day by day continuing with one mind in the temple, and breaking bread from house to house, they were taking their meals together with gladness and sincerity of heart.

The Greek says "simplicity of heart." Worship is basic and glad, not morbid and sophisticated. When you're finished worshiping, you should feel clean and fresh, ready to face the challenges God has placed before you.[8]

B. Instruction. A church is not only a worshiping community, it is a learning congregation. Verse 42a says:

> They were continually devoting themselves to the apostles' teaching.

Interestingly, that's first on the list. Why? Because babies need food. True, they need love and tenderness and cleansing. But they cry for food. Verse 44a goes on to inform us that "those who had believed were together." If we read between the lines of this verse, we find that there was something worth listening to, something to believe in, a body of truth to which they were committed. Similar passages are found in 4:4 and 6:4.

Benefits of Instruction

One of the marks of a healthy, growing church is the consistent, faithful instruction in the Word of God. Here are several benefits that come from regular teaching of the Word.

1. It gives substance to our faith.
2. It stabilizes us in times of testing.
3. It enables us to handle the Bible correctly, so we can nourish ourselves with its meat.
4. It equips us to detect and confront error.
5. It makes us confident in our walk.
6. It calms our fears and cancels our superstitions.

We must always keep in mind the primary purpose for our instruction: the glory of God. Knowledge is a wonderful thing, but knowledge alone can be dangerous (see 1 Cor. 8:1b, 11–12). When it remains theoretical, it breeds indifference. When it isn't balanced by love and grace, it breeds intolerance. When it becomes an end in itself, it breeds idolatry.

C. Fellowship. The early church was a caring flock, as revealed in Acts 2:44–45:

> And all those who had believed were together, and had all things in common; and they began selling their property and possessions, and were sharing them with all, as anyone might have need. (see also Acts 4:34–35)

8. Jesus said that the Father seeks our worship (John 4:23). Two excellent books that show you how to worship Him are: *Real Worship,* by Warren W. Wiersbe (Nashville, Tenn.: Oliver-Nelson Books, 1986); and *Worship,* by Evelyn Underhill (Evelyn Underhill, 1936; New York, N.Y.: Crossroad Publishing Co.).

D. Evangelism. The early church demonstrated its concern by reaching out to others. The people expressed the gospel in both word and deed—through missions, evangelism, and sharing their lives and possessions with the needy.

Activity versus Accomplishment

When the Crystal Palace Exhibition opened in 1851, people flocked to London's Hyde Park to behold the marvels. One of the greatest marvels back then was steam. Steam plows were displayed. Steam locomotives. Steam looms. Steam organs. Even a steam cannon.

Of all the great exhibits that year, the first-prize winner was a steam invention with seven thousand parts. When it was turned on, its pulleys, whistles, bells, and gears made a lot of noise, but, ironically, the contraption didn't do a thing! Seven thousand moving parts making a lot of commotion . . . but having no practical use.

With the high-tech era we live in, it's easy to confuse activity with accomplishment, to be fooled into thinking that the sound of gears and pulleys is the sound of something important being done.

Is that true of your life? Of your church? Are there hundreds, even thousands, of parts spinning and turning and making a lot of noise, but accomplishing very little?

If so, just remember that even though your contraption may win a prize at the state fair or the denominational convention, God is the final judge. And what you think has substance may dissipate before His searching eyes like steam.

Living Insights

Study One

The Bible portrays a local New Testament church for the first time in Acts 2:41–47. These verses hold the keys to unlocking the objectives of the church.

- Let's begin by paraphrasing this passage. Paraphrasing is rewriting the text in your own words. Through this beneficial exercise, you can get beyond the printed words and delve into the meanings and emotions of the text. Read between the lines as you work through the verses. Take your time and enjoy this study.

Continued on next page

Acts 2:41–47

Study Two

A large portion of this lesson is given to ten statements about the ministry. Because of their essential nature to this series, let's do some work to make them personal.

- Memorize the ten statements about the ministry. Write them on an index card and read them aloud. As you write and read the statements, you'll soon notice that you are less dependent on your notes. Keeping this list in your heart will help keep you on target in life!

A Closer Look at Our WIFE

Selected Scripture

A sign on the desk of a Pentagon official read: "The secrecy of my job does not permit me to know what I am doing." A similar sign could be placed on many a young minister's desk: "The sacredness of my job does not permit me to fully understand what I am doing."

The work of the church can become terribly complex and confusing. It's like mercury—difficult to get a grip on, and if mishandled, either the parishioner or the pastor is going to get hurt.

Although the ministry should be handled with respect, it shouldn't be handled covertly. Because sacredness is not to be confused with secrecy. As we learned in our last study, ministry should be open and aboveboard, with ten qualities that give it distinction. Let's review them.

1. The foundation of ministry is character—not professional skill.
2. The nature of ministry is service—not being served.
3. The motive for ministry is love—not money or power.
4. The measure of ministry is sacrifice—not success.
5. The authority of ministry is submission—not pulling rank.
6. The purpose of ministry is to glorify God—not to glorify ourselves.
7. The tools of ministry are prayer and Scripture—not a marketing handbook and an ingratiating manner.
8. The privilege of ministry is growth—which may be in depth rather than in numbers.
9. The power of ministry is the Holy Spirit—not programs.
10. The model for ministry is Jesus Christ—not a corporation or a man.[1]

Our primary purpose in all we do in the ministry should be to glorify God. It is only right that this should be our goal, for God is the one

> Who created the heavens and stretched them out,
> Who spread out the earth and its offspring,
> Who gives breath to the people on it,
> And spirit to those who walk in it. (Isa. 42:5)

James gives us the practical ramifications of Isaiah's verses: "If the Lord wills, we shall live and also do this or that" (James 4:15). He is sovereign.

1. Warren W. Wiersbe and David Wiersbe, *Making Sense of the Ministry* (Chicago, Ill.: Moody Press, 1983), pp. 31–46.

His responsibility is to rule; ours is to submit. And as Isaiah continues to point out, this Sovereign will not share His glory with His subjects.

> "I am the Lord, I have called you in righteousness,
> I will also hold you by the hand and watch over you,
> And I will appoint you as a covenant to the people,
> As a light to the nations,
> To open blind eyes,
> To bring out prisoners from the dungeon,
> And those who dwell in darkness from the prison.
> I am the Lord, that is My name;
> I will not give My glory to another,
> Nor My praise to graven images." (Isa. 42:6–8)

These are easily forgotten words in a growing, dynamic church where God's blessing currently rests. Sadly, after many in the ministry have attained a certain skill and following, they seek *their* glory instead of God's. But we must always remember that we are to seek great things for God—not ourselves (compare Jer. 45:5a). As we turn to the growing, dynamic church of the first century, we will see how God's glory is worked out.

I. A Brief Glance Backward

Woven into the fabric of the scriptural tapestry in Acts 2 are four pictures of meaningful activities the early church was involved in. As we noted in the last lesson, these pictures form the acronym *WIFE.*

- *W* stands for worship. The early church was a worshiping community (v. 42; see also v. 43).
- *I* stands for instruction. The early church was a learning congregation (v. 42; see also 4:4, 5:42, 6:4).
- *F* stands for fellowship. The early church was a caring flock (2:44–45).
- *E* stands for evangelism. The early church was a reaching body (v. 47).

Spiritual Starvation

Famine is a grotesque and global reality. We've all seen heart-wrenching pictures of starving, emaciated children with their spindly legs and protruding bellies.

But the prophet Amos describes another, more acute famine—a famine of the soul.

> "The time is surely coming," says the Lord God, "when I will send a famine on the land—not a famine of bread or water, but of hearing the words of the Lord. Men will wander everywhere from sea to sea, seeking the Word of the Lord, searching, running here and going there, but will not find it. Beautiful

girls and fine young men alike will grow faint and weary, thirsting for the Word of God." (Amos 8:11–13)[2]

That is the spiritual condition of most people in the world. They are starving for truth. Their energies are wasted; their trust, waning; their hope, withered. They don't know where to turn when the bottom drops out. Or which direction to take when their lives are at a crossroads. Lost in a desert, they look desperately for an oasis of truth.

Remember that the next time you're tempted to criticize the church you attend. Stop and think about the refreshment of worship, the nourishment of spiritual food, the shade of fellowship. Then, instead of harping and haranguing, humble yourself and give thanks for what you've got. Because whether your church is a small fruit tree or a sprawling oasis, it's helping to keep you alive.

II. A Closer Look Inward

We examined worship and instruction in the previous lesson. Now let's take a closer look at the objectives of fellowship and evangelism.

A. The value of fellowship. From Acts 2:42, we see that the early church devoted itself to fellowship. The Greek word *koinōnia,* with the root *koinos,* has the idea of something being held "in common."[3] That's the thought of verse 44.

> And all those who had believed were together, and had all things in common.

The New Testament church not only had things in common together, they *were* together. Not like a bunch of isolated marbles that made a lot of noise and scattered in all directions, but like a cluster of grapes. And when the winepress of persecution came squeezing down on them, this close body of believers bled together. Out of this painful, crushing experience came the sweet wine of fellowship. We might define fellowship as "expressions of genuine Christianity, freely shared among God's members." In the New Testament there are two definite expressions of fellowship. The first is to share some *thing* with someone else; the second, to share *in* something with someone else. The former sense is used in verse 45.

2. The Living Bible (Wheaton, Ill.: Tyndale House Publishers, 1971).

3. *Koinōnia* is used twenty times in the New Testament and its related terms, another nineteen. Almost without exception, the meaning involves sharing. For example, in Luke 5:10 business partners were called *koinōnos.* Hebrews 10:33 talks about being sharers in suffering. And Galatians 2:9 speaks of "the right hand of fellowship" as *koinōnia.*

And they began selling their property and possessions, and were sharing[4] them with all, as anyone might have need.

In verses 44–45, the word *all* appears three times. *Koinōnia* was not an esoteric function of the clergy; it included everyone.

B. The importance of evangelism. As we read verses 43–47, it is clear that the quality of fellowship drew people into the church rather than drove them away.

> And the Lord was adding to their number day by day those who were being saved. (v. 47b)

People came to the church because the gospel was taken into the streets to them. Acts 3:1–8 recounts one such expression of the early church's faith.

> Now Peter and John were going up to the temple at the ninth hour, the hour of prayer. And a certain man who had been lame from his mother's womb was being carried along, whom they used to set down every day at the gate of the temple which is called Beautiful, in order to beg alms of those who were entering the temple. And when he saw Peter and John about to go into the temple, he began asking to receive alms. And Peter, along with John, fixed his gaze upon him and said, "Look at us!" And he began to give them his attention, expecting to receive something from them. But Peter said, "I do not possess silver and gold, but what I do have I give to you: In the name of Jesus Christ the Nazarene—walk!" And seizing him by the right hand, he raised him up; and immediately his feet and his ankles were strengthened. And with a leap, he stood upright and began to walk; and he entered the temple with them, walking and leaping and praising God.

Peter and John were in the streets of Jerusalem, which gave them an opportunity to minister to one in need. This led to a perfect opportunity to speak publicly about Christ (vv. 11–26), which, in turn, led to opposition.

> And as they were speaking to the people, the priests and the captain of the temple guard, and the Sadducees, came upon them, being greatly disturbed because they were teaching the people and proclaiming in Jesus the resurrection from the dead. And they laid hands on them, and put them in jail until the next day, for it was already evening. (4:1–3)

4. "Sharing" is *koinōnia* in the original Greek.

The work of evangelism, though, continued.

> But many of those who had heard the message believed; and the number of the men came to be about five thousand. (v. 4)

Even incarceration could not confine Peter's expression of faith (see vv. 7–14). In chapter 5, a similar scene occurs. Another arrest. Another threatening event.

> And when they had brought them, they stood them before the Council. And the high priest questioned them, saying, "We gave you strict orders not to continue teaching in this name, and behold, you have filled Jerusalem with your teaching, and intend to bring this man's blood upon us." But Peter and the apostles answered and said, "We must obey God rather than men." (vv. 27–29)

And then Peter preaches in verses 30–32, with the result found in verse 33.

> But when they heard this, they were cut to the quick and were intending to slay them.

Gamaliel, a Pharisee, intercedes in verses 34–39, saying that if this movement were of men, the apostles' mission would grind to a halt on its own; but if it were a mission from God, then the Pharisees were fighting against God and wouldn't be able to stop it. The Council accepted Gamaliel's words.

> And they took his advice; and after calling the apostles in, they flogged them and ordered them to speak no more in the name of Jesus, and then released them. So they went on their way from the presence of the Council, rejoicing that they had been considered worthy to suffer shame for His name. And every day, in the temple and from house to house, they kept right on teaching and preaching Jesus as the Christ. (vv. 40–42)

The message went out . . . ever reaching . . . ever effective . . . ever motivating. The result? Growth![5] And to this day, growth continues. For Acts, the Bible's only "unfinished book," is still being written in the lives of men and women today.

Evangelism in the New Testament

We can make four observations about evangelism in the New Testament. First, *it was never limited to the church facilities.* In fact, it seldom occurred in a place of worship.

5. See Acts 6:1a, 11:19–24.

Most often, it took place in streets, jails, and homes. Second, *it was always initiated by the Christian.* People didn't come to the church to find Christ; Christians took Christ into the world to find people. Third, *it was usually connected with another unrelated event or experience*—a healing, an imprisonment, a conversation, a need, which led naturally to the issue of Jesus Christ. Fourth, *people were not forced into it.* Never once was an unsaved person manipulated into believing. They were treated with dignity, with respect, with intelligence.

How different from the way evangelism is often carried out today. Caring for people, helping them, and being genuinely involved in their lives is still the ideal entrée to express our faith.

Because people will never care how much we know until they know how much we care.

III. A Realistic Look Forward

We've looked backward and inward; now it's time to look forward.

A. The depth of a church is determined by the quality of its worship and instruction. We can't give up worship because we believe in instruction. Neither should we stop teaching because we love to worship. Rather, it is the quality of *both* worship and education that gives a church strength, stability, and discernment.

B. The breadth of a church is determined by its commitment to fellowship and evangelism. If we stop evangelizing, we will become an exclusive clique instead of a caring church. If we don't reach out, we will become ingrown.

The Responsibility of Love

Love has a hem to her garment
That trails in the very dust;
It can reach the stains of the streets and the lanes . . .
And because it can, it must.

—Anonymous

Living Insights

Study One

We've returned to Acts 2:41–47 as the basis for our study. These verses are loaded with gold nuggets, so let's explore yet another approach to this text.

- We often miss key concepts because we're too familiar with the words. This time, read Acts 2:41–47 in another version of the New Testament. You might try the New King James, New American Standard, Revised Standard, New International, or maybe a paraphrase like The Living Bible or Phillips's New Testament in Modern English. Ask God to show you something fresh during this time in His Word.

Living Insights

Study Two

Now that you know what WIFE means in this lesson, how is *your* WIFE? Are you experiencing a vibrant, aggressive, joyful time in all four areas of church activity? Or do you give yourself a mixed review?

- Evaluate your participation in the following areas, with 1 being lowest and 5, highest. Remember, this isn't an evaluation of your church; it's an evaluation of *your participation* in your church.

Worship	1	2	3	4	5
Instruction	1	2	3	4	5
Fellowship	1	2	3	4	5
Evangelism	1	2	3	4	5

A Church with a Contagious Style

1 Thessalonians 2:1–13

Just as you cannot tell a book by its cover, so you cannot tell a church by its building. As a matter of fact, buildings are a rather poor basis of judgment.

It's often difficult for us to see beyond the surface. We look at a large, urban church and assume it's cold and unfriendly. And when we look at a small church nestled in a clump of trees out in the country, well kept and attractive, we tend to assume it's a warm, welcoming community of people. Or when we see a church covered with ivy and marked with age, our tendency is to think it's probably well rooted in the Scriptures. Not necessarily. Looks can be deceiving.

When Jesus spoke to Peter in Matthew 16:18, He gave us not only a prediction about the church but also a wonderful promise. The prediction: "I will build My church." The promise: "The gates of Hades shall not overpower it." Jesus did not have in mind a place; He had in mind a people. In fact, the word translated *church* literally means "called out." Jesus is saying that those who are called out from the world, now and in the years to come, will stand as a monument to Him. They will be so invincible that even the demons from hell will not be able to overpower, overthrow, or obliterate them.

In a fine little book titled *The Church of the Catacombs,* Walter Oetting writes:

> If you had asked, "Where is the church?" in any important city of the ancient world where Christianity had penetrated in the first century, you would have been directed to a group of worshiping people gathered in a house. There was no special building or other tangible wealth with which to associate "church," only people![1]

I. Various Types of Churches

Not until the turn of the first century did churches begin to build buildings. By the third century, the buildings were emphasized more than the people. In the book *The Problem of Wineskins,* the author has divided existing churches into four main categories:

1. *The Body Church.* This type is closest to the New Testament experience. It holds no property and needs none. It arranges its worship gatherings according to

1. Walter Oetting, *The Church of the Catacombs,* rev. ed. (St. Louis, Mo.: Concordia Publishing House, 1970), p. 25.

available space in homes, schools, rented halls or other facilities. Its structure is largely organic, based on a network of small groups bound together by large-group corporate worship experiences. . . .

2. *The Cathedral Church.* Regardless of the size of its building, such a church really sees the building as *the church,* and it is the building which determines the church's whole program and lifestyle. . . .
3. *The Tabernacle Church.* This church has a building, but the building is strictly secondary and functional. It is not a "holy place" in any inherent sense, but is seen as a facility to be used to extend the kingdom of God. The building may be large or small, simple or elaborate. The important thing is that it is functional. It is built for flexibility and multiple use. . . .
4. *The Phantom Church.* This final type prides itself on having no building. The problem is, it has very little structure of any kind! It is like a Rorschach ink blot: Each person makes what he wants of it.[2]

II. Four Faces of a Contagious Style

Far more significant than structure or size is the *style* of a church, a fact Paul brings out in 1 Thessalonians 2:1–13. Paul's opening remark concerns his evaluation of his ministry among them.

> For you yourselves know, brethren, that our coming to you was not in vain. (v. 1)

The word *vain* means "empty . . . without result, without profit, without effect, without reaching its goal." Whenever Paul thought of the church at Thessalonica, he thought of it in purposeful and productive terms, never as empty or hollow. Although verse 1 sounds like a honeymoon for a pastor, verse 2 indicates it was far from that.

> But after we had already suffered and been mistreated in Philippi, as you know, we had the boldness in our God to speak to you the gospel of God amid much opposition.

The church at Thessalonica was a church that was born—and grew—amidst opposition. As we scan the passage, the contagious style of this church becomes evident.

A. Biblical in content. Again and again, whenever Paul recalls the Thessalonican church, his memories center around the content of his ministry—the gospel.

> We had the boldness in our God to speak to you *the gospel* of God amid much opposition. . . . But just as

2. Howard A. Snyder, *The Problem of Wineskins* (Downers Grove, Ill.: InterVarsity Press, 1975), pp. 75–77.

> we have been approved by God to be entrusted with *the gospel,* so we speak, not as pleasing men but God, who examines our hearts.... Having thus a fond affection for you, we were well-pleased to impart to you not only *the gospel* of God but also our own lives, because you had become very dear to us. For you recall, brethren, our labor and hardship, how working night and day so as not to be a burden to any of you, we proclaimed to you *the gospel* of God.... And for this reason we also constantly thank God that when you received from us *the word of God's message,* you accepted it not as the word of men, but for what it really is, *the word of God,* which also performs its work in you who believe. (vv. 2b–13, emphasis added)

That's the first face of a contagious style: *it's biblical in content.* When you came to the church at Thessalonica, you heard the Word of God—not the opinions of a preacher. And notice in verse 3 how pure that Word was.

> For our exhortation does not come from error or impurity or by way of deceit.

God's Word cuts the heart out of hypocrisy and keeps us from deceit and impurity. It also helps the pastor to think less about pleasing his flock and more about presenting God's Word.

> But just as we have been approved by God to be entrusted with the gospel, so we speak, not as pleasing men but God, who examines our hearts. (v. 4)

Just as a parent carefully plans and prepares nourishing meals for the family instead of junk food, so the pastor carefully feeds his flock. John R. W. Stott speaks about this in his book *The Preacher's Portrait:*

> It is not enough for the preacher to know the Word of God; he must know the people to whom he proclaims it. He must not, of course, falsify God's Word in order to make it more appealing. He cannot dilute the strong medicine of Scripture to render it more sweet to the taste. But he may seek to present it to the people in such a way as to commend it to them. For one thing, he will make it simple. This surely is what Paul meant when he told Timothy to be 'a workman who has no need to be ashamed, rightly handling the word of truth' (2 Tim. 2:15). The verb, [rightly handling], means literally, 'cutting straight'. It was employed of road making and is, for instance, used in the [Septuagint] of Proverbs 3:6: 'He will make

straight [A.V., "direct"] your paths'. Our exposition of the Scripture is to be so simple and direct, so easily intelligible, that it resembles a straight road. It is easy to follow it. . . . The expository preacher is a bridge builder, seeking to span the gulf between the Word of God and the mind of man. He must do his utmost to interpret the Scripture so accurately and plainly, and to apply it so forcefully, that the truth crosses the bridge. . . .

But wherein does the preacher's authority lie? The preacher's authority is not that of the prophet. . . . Instead, our formula, if we use one at all, should be the well-known, oft-repeated and quite proper phrase of Dr. Billy Graham, 'The Bible says'.

This is real authority.[3]

A church that remains biblical in content will become known as a place that tells the truth . . . that establishes its convictions on the bedrock of God's voice of authority, not on the shifting sands of human opinion.

B. Authentic in nature. In verses 5–6, the emphasis shifts from the message to the messenger.

For we never came with flattering speech, as you know, nor with a pretext for greed—God is witness—nor did we seek glory from men, either from you or from others, even though as apostles of Christ we might have asserted our authority.

Paul didn't use flattery as a method or greed as a motivation, nor did he exploit his flock or use them for his own self-aggrandizement. Also, Paul refused the world's way of "winning by intimidation"—he didn't pull rank on his parishioners. Instead of leaning on his apostolic authority, he relied on the authenticity of his message. First Corinthians 2 underscores this approach.

And when I came to you, brethren, I did not come with superiority of speech or of wisdom, proclaiming to you the testimony of God. . . . I was with you in weakness and in fear and in much trembling. And my message and my preaching were not in persuasive words of wisdom, but in demonstration of the Spirit and of power, that your faith should not rest on the wisdom of men, but on the power of God. (vv. 1–5)

3. John R. W. Stott, *The Preacher's Portrait: Some New Testament Word Studies* (Grand Rapids, Mich.: William B. Eerdmans Publishing Co., 1961), pp. 28–29.

Authentic Christianity

Authenticity occurs when real people say real things about real issues with real feelings. Living what you are . . . telling the truth . . . admitting your failures and weaknesses—that's how you stay real.

May we ask a few searching questions: How real are you? Does an authentic life back up your words?

Take a look at flattery. If that's a part of your life, get rid of it.

How about greed? Is there an ulterior motive lurking behind all your decisions and conversations? If so, get rid of it.

Do you seek your own glory, the praise of other people? If so, get rid of that motivation.

Do you exploit your authority as a parent? As a partner? As a pastor? If so, get rid of that self-serving habit—and get real!

C. **Gracious in attitude.** The third face of a church with a contagious style is graciousness.

> But we proved to be gentle among you, as a nursing mother tenderly cares for her own children. Having thus a fond affection for you, we were well-pleased to impart to you not only the gospel of God but also our own lives, because you had become very dear to us. For you recall, brethren, our labor and hardship, how working night and day so as not to be a burden to any of you, we proclaimed to you the gospel of God. You are witnesses, and so is God, how devoutly and uprightly and blamelessly we behaved toward you believers; just as you know how we were exhorting and encouraging and imploring each one of you as a father would his own children. (1 Thess. 2:7–11)

This passage is like a pair of parentheses. The opening parenthesis is as a mother, the closing parenthesis, as a father. This implies that the church is a family, not a business. It's a family of people held together by common beliefs: that Jesus is Lord and God, that He died for our sins, that He has risen from the dead and lives forever, and that He waits to gather us to Himself in glory. All of this by a common faith apart from works. This core of the Christian faith isn't open for interpretation or opinion. It's settled. But how do we deal with people who are struggling to understand the essence of the Christian faith? The answer is found in verses 7–11: with grace.

Gracious Christianity

Instead of being harsh and demanding, Paul was gentle and tolerant. Instead of sounding like an officer, he was like a tenderly nursing mother. Instead of coming down with strong commands, he exhibited fond affection. Instead of imparting only truth, he imparted his own life as well. Instead of seeing the Thessalonians as dry sponges that just needed to soak up truth, he told them how dear they had become to him. Instead of taking advantage of them, he worked day and night so as not to be a burden. Instead of living selfishly, he behaved blamelessly, like a father with his family.

These words drip with compassion, tact, and tenderness. Is that how you act with those who are struggling? Are those the attitudes that underlie your actions?

Carl Sandburg, describing Abraham Lincoln, called him a man of steel and velvet. On February 12, 1959, Sandburg referred to him in these terms:

> Not often in the story of mankind does a man arrive on earth who is both steel and velvet, who is as hard as rock and soft as drifting fog, who holds in his heart and mind the paradox of terrible storm and peace unspeakable and perfect....
>
> While the war winds howled, he insisted that the Mississippi was one river meant to belong to one country....
>
> While the luck of war wavered and broke and came again, as generals failed and campaigns were lost, he held enough forces ... together to raise new armies and supply them, until generals were found who made war as victorious war has always been made, with terror, frightfulness, destruction ... valor and sacrifice past words of man to tell.
>
> In the mixed shame and blame of the immense wrongs of two crashing civilizations, often with nothing to say, he said nothing, slept not at all, and on occasions he was seen to weep in a way that made weeping appropriate, decent, majestic.[4]

A man of steel and velvet. A man like Paul was. A man like we should be.

4. Charles R. Swindoll, *Leadership* (Waco, Tex.: Word Books, 1985), pp. 61–62.

D. Relevant in approach. Paul's approach to ministry was biblical in content, authentic in nature, gracious in attitude, and finally, relevant in approach.

> So that you may walk in a manner worthy of the God who calls you into His own kingdom and glory. And for this reason we also constantly thank God that when you received from us the word of God's message, you accepted it not as the word of men, but for what it really is, the word of God, which also performs its work in you who believe. (vv. 12–13)

That's relevance—a message with today's issues in mind. Paul's approach never compartmentalizes the sacred from the secular . . . it touches all of life. The way you conduct your business is no less sacred than the way you conduct your worship. Christ penetrates all of it. Jesus penetrated life's streets—not so much its sanctuaries. He met politicians as politicians, beggars as beggars, the blind as blind, prostitutes as prostitutes. He met their needs at those particular moments. And He met them where they were.

Taking the Cross Out of the Cathedral

George MacLeod wrote a poem that helps put a lot of things in perspective, helping to emphasize content rather than cosmetics, Christ rather than self, the gospel going beyond the church walls rather than simply being contained within them.

> I simply argue that the cross be raised again
> at the center of the market place
> as well as on the steeple of the church,
> I am recovering the claim that
> Jesus was not crucified in a cathedral
> between two candles:
> But on a cross between two thieves;
> on a town garbage heap;
> At a crossroad of politics so cosmopolitan
> that they had to write His title
> in Hebrew and in Latin and in Greek . . .
> And at the kind of place where cynics talk smut,
> and thieves curse and soldiers gamble.
> Because that is where He died,
> and that is what He died about.
> And that is where Christ's men ought to be,
> and what church people ought to be about.[5]

5. Charles R. Swindoll, *Strengthening Your Grip* (Waco, Tex.: Word Books, 1982), p. 26.

III. When That Style Occurs

When this contagious style occurs in our lives and in our churches, what can we expect? We can expect that God will honor our efforts, regardless of our weaknesses and imperfections. We can expect that we will model first-century Christlikeness in twentieth-century style. And we can expect that others will desire to join us, in spite of the difficulties. The secret to this style is to keep the right perspective: to place more emphasis on content and less on cosmetics; to do more exalting of Christ and less of one another; to remind ourselves more that the church is made up of people, not structures; and to take the gospel outside the church walls, not just enjoy it within them.

Living Insights

Study One

Paul's comments in 1 Thessalonians 2 are exciting, enthusiastic, even contagious! Yet it's important to ask *why*. What is it in this text that conveys such a positive feeling? Let's look for the answer by examining the key words.

- Reread 1 Thessalonians 2:1–13, and jot down twelve to fifteen key words from the text. Then try to define the words from the passage itself. If that isn't possible, consult a good Bible dictionary. After you've recorded a working definition of the word, conclude by writing a phrase or sentence that explains why the word is significant.

1 Thessalonians 2:1–13

Key word: ____________________

Definition: ____

Significance: ____

____

Key word: ____________________

Definition: ____

Significance: ____

____

Continued on next page

Key word: ____________________

Definition: ____

Significance: ____

____

Key word: ____________________

Definition: ____

Significance: ____

____

Key word: ____________________

Definition: ____

Significance: ____

____

Key word: ____________________

Definition: ____

Significance: ____

____

Key word: ____________________

Definition: ____

Significance: ____

____

Key word: ____________________

Definition: ____

Significance: ____

____

Key word: ____________________

Definition: ____

Significance: ____

____

Key word: ____________________

Definition: ____

Significance: ____

____

Key word: ____________________

Definition: ____

Significance: ____

____

Key word: ____________________

Definition: ____

Significance: ____

____

Key word: ____________________

Definition: ____

Significance: ____

____

Key word: ____________________

Definition: ____

Significance: ____

____

Continued on next page

Key word: ____________________

Definition: ____

Significance: ____

____

Living Insights

Study Two

Are you part of a church with a contagious style? Is it biblical, authentic, gracious, and relevant? If so, you have much to be thankful for. If not, change can occur . . . starting with you!

- Let's commit these issues to prayer. If your church has a contagious style, thank the Lord for allowing you to be a part of it. If it needs some help, ask the Lord to cause the change to begin with you. There's no need to make this a public display. Just make it a matter of prayer between you and God. Be sensitive to how He will use you in the days ahead.

Analysis of a Metropolitan Ministry

Exodus 18:7–24, Ephesians 4:11–16

The big church has taken a bum rap. Down through the years, especially in this generation, it seems as though size alone makes you suspect. That's rather curious, because it's not true in secular organizations.

For example, in the domestic realm, big families are usually admired and esteemed. That's also true of stores and companies. The bigger stores offer more options and often at better prices. The larger companies like IBM, General Motors, and AT&T have the ability to do extensive research, set standards, and supply state-of-the-art products and services. If you need hospital care, you'd probably choose a large, well-established, modern place over a struggling little clinic. In air travel, no one's going to take a single-engine, long-distance flight that dusts crops along the way. Academic pursuits are no different. Most people would prefer a larger school with extensive facilities and faculty rather than a school with three on the faculty, two of which are part-time.

But for some reason, people don't look at the church that way. Whenever a church gets big, people get suspicious. They think it's an ego trip for the pastor or that the church is just concerned with buildings and numbers.

As we turn our attention to the early church, however, we find that the very first local church was a large organization.

> So then, those who had received his word were baptized; and there were added that day about three thousand souls. (Acts 2:41)

To this already large number, God kept adding new converts.

> And the Lord was adding to their number day by day those who were being saved. (v. 47b)

By the fourth chapter, the numbers constituted a very large church indeed.

> But many of those who had heard the message believed; and the number of the men came to be about five thousand. (v. 4)

But, like any large church, it had its problems.

> Now at this time while the disciples were increasing in number, a complaint arose on the part of the Hellenistic Jews against the native Hebrews, because their widows were being overlooked in the daily serving of food. And the twelve summoned the congregation of the disciples and said, "It is not desirable

> for us to neglect the word of God in order to serve tables. But select from among you, brethren, seven men of good reputation, full of the Spirit and of wisdom, whom we may put in charge of this task. But we will devote ourselves to prayer, and to the ministry of the word." (6:1–4)

Some of the church members were saying that the leadership was unconcerned and lacked compassion for the needy widows. But nothing could be further from the truth. Supplying food for the widows was a pressing priority, but these men had a higher priority—spiritually feeding the church so that the members might take up the work of ministry, which included the ministry of meals for widows.

I. A Metropolitan Ministry: Neither New nor Novel

In recent history as well, large, metropolitan churches have been on the scene for years. Carr's Lane Congregational Church was a busy, nineteenth-century urban ministry in Birmingham, England, pastored for thirty-six years by R. W. Dale and later by John Henry Jowett. Saint Paul's was a large, famous church pastored by Henry Liddon. Then there was the sizable City Temple in London, pastored by Joseph Parker. It was second only in size to London's famed, six-thousand-member Metropolitan Tabernacle, pastored by Charles Haddon Spurgeon. On the other side of the Atlantic, in Boston, evangelist Dwight L. Moody also preached to a congregation of six thousand and to thousands more in churches across the country. Then there's Moody Church in Chicago, Tenth Presbyterian Church in Philadelphia pastored for thirty-three years by Donald Barnhouse, and the Church of the Open Door in Los Angeles pastored by J. Vernon McGee for more than twenty years. The list goes on and on.[1] Metropolitan churches have always been around and have made an undeniable impact. Often these large, progressive churches set trends, change directions, and implement innovations. Yet, in spite of the benefits, large churches are not without their organizational and managerial problems.

Size Can Be Deceiving

Bigger is not always better.

A big church can become a fat, lazy giant that lumbers in and out of the pews week after week, dozing off right after the

1. "Approximately 1 percent of all the Protestant churches on this continent average more than 700 at worship on Sunday morning, but together the approximately 3,500 congregations in this category account for at least 7 percent of all the Protestant worshipers on the typical Sabbath. In our classification system these "super-churches" or "mini-denominations" resemble autonomous nations. . . . By definition a nation is an independent entity. It has its own distinctive history and its own culture, and it acts as an autonomous community with its own leaders." Lyle E. Schaller, *Looking in the Mirror* (Nashville, Tenn.: Abingdon Press, 1984), pp. 32–33.

doxology. But with the right encouragement, that sleeping giant can be awakened. And with huge strides it can move out into the community and make an enormous impact.

But if your church is small, as are most churches, don't be intimidated. You, too, can make an equally important impact for Christ. Remember, it was not a huge Israelite army that turned the tide in the battle with the Philistines; it was a shepherd boy named David, with only five smooth stones and a slingshot.

II. Various Principles for Keeping the Ministry Effective

In today's lesson, we will address these organizational and managerial problems from two passages of Scripture, Exodus 18 and Ephesians 4.

A. From Moses' experience. Moses had come to his calling from spending forty years with sheep. Life had been simple, tasks predictable and repetitive, and he'd had sufficient time to maintain priorities. Suddenly he found himself as "senior pastor" of the "Wilderness Tabernacle." On him the people placed enormous respect, and also enormous expectations. Realizing that Moses would not last long in such a setting without crumbling, God sent a consultant to him—his father-in-law, Jethro. Exodus 18:7 tells us that the reunion was warm.

> Then Moses went out to meet his father-in-law, and he bowed down and kissed him; and they asked each other of their welfare, and went into the tent.

Verse 8 records the pastor's glowing report.

> And Moses told his father-in-law all that the Lord had done to Pharaoh and to the Egyptians for Israel's sake, all the hardship that had befallen them on the journey, and how the Lord had delivered them.

In verses 9–12, we see that the consultant's response was jubilant.

> And Jethro rejoiced over all the goodness which the Lord had done to Israel, in delivering them from the hand of the Egyptians. So Jethro said, "Blessed be the Lord who delivered you from the hand of the Egyptians and from the hand of Pharaoh, and who delivered the people from under the hand of the Egyptians. Now I know that the Lord is greater than all the gods; indeed, it was proven when they dealt proudly against the people." Then Jethro, Moses' father-in-law, took a burnt offering and sacrifices for God, and Aaron came with all the elders of Israel to eat a meal with Moses' father-in-law before God.

But the fuller reality of the situation revealed itself the next day. Moses was up to his ears in court cases.

> And it came about the next day that Moses sat to judge the people, and the people stood about Moses from the morning until the evening. Now when Moses' father-in-law saw all that he was doing for the people, he said, "What is this thing that you are doing for the people? Why do you alone sit as judge and all the people stand about you from morning until evening?" And Moses said to his father-in-law, "Because the people come to me to inquire of God. When they have a dispute, it comes to me, and I judge between a man and his neighbor, and make known the statutes of God and His laws." (vv. 13–16)

Moses had the right motive in serving the people; he simply had the wrong method. And it took a firm father-in-law to steer him onto the right track.

> And Moses' father-in-law said to him, "The thing that you are doing is not good.[2] You will surely wear out,[3] both yourself and these people who are with you, for the task is too heavy for you; you cannot do it alone." (vv. 17–18)

The consultant hadn't made his observation hurriedly. He watched (v. 14a), then questioned (v. 14b), then listened as Moses answered (vv. 15–16). Finally, Jethro advised him that he couldn't do it *alone* (v. 18). Moses felt indispensable, an illusion Jethro quickly dispelled. But Jethro didn't stand back and throw rocks at Moses either. Instead, he put a firm but gentle arm around Moses' shoulders.

> "Furthermore, you shall select out of all the people able men who fear God, men of truth, those who hate dishonest gain; and you shall place these over them, as leaders of thousands, of hundreds, of fifties and of tens. And let them judge the people at all times; and let it be that every major dispute they will bring to you, but every minor dispute they themselves will judge. So it will be easier for you, and they will bear the burden with you." (vv. 21–22; compare Acts 6:3–4)

The results were fourfold for Moses: the ministry would be easier, others would feel they were a significant part of the ministry,

2. The Hebrew sentence is emphatic, beginning with the words *not good:* "Not good is the thing you are doing."

3. The Hebrew for "wear out" suggests that Moses would become old and exhausted before his time, dying an earlier death. And not only him, but the people as well.

he would live longer, and it would work—people's needs would be met.

> "If you do this thing and God so commands you, then you will be able to endure, and all these people also will go to their place in peace." So Moses listened to his father-in-law, and did all that he had said. (Exod. 18:23–24)

How does this apply to a metropolitan ministry? First of all, *many people plus high expectations plus numerous needs equals endless responsibilities.* That equation must be evaluated by both clergy and laity. Second, *as work increases, the load must be shifted.* In a word, *delegation.* Efficiency is increased not so much by what one accomplishes, but by what one relinquishes. Third, *God's servants are not exempt from the penalties of breaking God's natural laws.* Pastors, like anybody else, can get ulcers, have emotional problems, lose their wives and families, and die young. Every metropolitan ministry must evaluate where it is going and what it is doing. Are responsibilities distributed equally? If not, both clergy and congregation will suffer.

B. From Paul's perspective. Ephesians 4 speaks to this issue of how to run the ministry without wearing out the minister. The secret in organizing a church is to maximize its efficiency by delegating the work to qualified, gifted people. This is the thrust of verses 11–16. From this passage, several principles emerge.

1. **There are sufficient gifts within the church body to sustain any church.**

   > And He gave some as apostles, and some as prophets, and some as evangelists, and some as pastors and teachers, for the equipping of the saints for the work of service, to the building up of the body of Christ. (vv. 11–12)[4]

2. **When these gifts are exercised, congregations "grow up."**

   > Until we all attain to the unity of the faith, and of the knowledge of the Son of God, to a mature man, to the measure of the stature which belongs to the fulness of Christ. As a result, we are no longer to be children, tossed here and there by waves, and carried about by every wind of doctrine, by the trickery of men, by craftiness in deceitful scheming; but speaking the truth in love, we are to grow up in all aspects into Him, who is the head, even Christ. (vv. 13–15)

4. Other lists of spiritual gifts can be found in Romans 12, 1 Corinthians 12, and 1 Peter 4.

3. **Maximum involvement leads to healthy growth.**

From whom the whole body, being fitted and held together by that which every joint supplies, according to the proper working of each individual part, causes the growth of the body for the building up of itself in love. (v. 16)

III. An Understanding of the Major Differences

The small, neighborhood concept of ministry and the large, metropolitan concept represent contrasting philosophies. The chart at the end of the lesson helps to clarify these distinctive types of ministry.

IV. It's Helpful to Keep in Mind That . . .

First: If you have neighborhood expectations, you will be frustrated in metropolitan churches—expecting close ties with the senior pastor, expecting others to know you personally, and expecting instant and intimate attention. *Second:* Broad-minded flexibility and small-group participation are major secrets of survival for a healthy metropolitan church. Don't expect your own seat or parking space. Be willing to accept a position of lay leadership and supervision. Be flexible in adapting to different ministry styles and music. *Third:* Changing methods doesn't mean a changing message.

Family Ties

So much responsibility is on *your* shoulders. Just like in a big family, some of the kids help to raise the babies, right? Talk to people who are raised in large families. The older ones change the diapers and help with the cooking. The middle ones help with the washing. And they all help with the cleaning. That's just part of being in a big family. Otherwise, Mom goes crazy because she can't keep up with it all.

Are you part of a church family? If so, are you pitching in, doing your fair share? Are you giving your time, your prayers, your gifts, your financial support? And are you giving them faithfully and cheerfully?

Philosophies in Contrast

The "Neighborhood" Concept	*The "Metropolitan" Concept*
1. Close ties between pastor and people—"one big family . . . identify with the pastor"	1. Close ties between identity group—"numerous families . . . identify with one another"
2. Smaller scale: staff . . . vision . . . organization . . . facilities . . . budget . . . outreach . . . provisions . . . variety	2. Larger scale: staff . . . vision . . . organization . . . facilities . . . budget . . . outreach . . . provisions . . . variety
3. Congregation drawn mainly from <u>close</u> radius	3. Congregation drawn from <u>vast</u> radius
4. Tendency to be "inbred" . . . narrow rotation among lay leadership . . . greater reticence to change	4. Less "inbred" . . . broad rotation among lay leadership . . . less reticence to change
5. Easy to know everyone	5. Impossible to know everyone
6. Workload borne by volunteers	6. Some work delegated to specialists
7. Relatively simple to manage and maintain	7. Complex to manage and maintain
8. One-man operation . . . more rigid control	8. Multi-staff . . . team emphasis among all in leadership . . . broader base of control
9. Strong, centralized loyalty to "the church" . . . easier to implement involvement	9. Loyalty decentralized to various ministries . . . more difficult to implement involvement
10. Atmosphere naturally warm and friendly	10. Atmosphere can still be warm and friendly—but a constant challenge

Living Insights

Study One

Throughout the centuries, biblical scholars have understood Jethro's advice in Exodus 18 in two different ways. Some feel Jethro's intentions were good, but his advice wasn't. Thus, they feel Moses erred in following his father-in-law's suggestions. Other students feel that Jethro's advice was sound and Moses was wise to heed it. Let us help you make up your own mind by providing you with a few questions to answer.

- Are there any clues within Exodus 18:17–24 that point toward good advice or bad?
- What about the surrounding context, verses 1–16 and chapter 19? Any help there?
- Are there other Scripture passages that address these issues?
- What are some of the arguments for Jethro giving bad advice?
- What are some of the arguments for Jethro giving good advice?

Living Insights

Study Two

This study mostly concentrated on the size of a local church. Let's continue to personalize this series by thinking about your local church.

- Would you call your church large, medium, or small?
- What are the advantages of attending your church?
- Are there any disadvantages?
- Would you say you're experiencing maximum involvement in your church?
- How could you improve your relationship with your church?

Changing Times—Changeless Truths

Selected Scripture

"The good old days."

Almost every week we meet people who long for them, for a return to the past—when a haircut cost two bits, when there was no such thing as an energy crisis, when the air was clean, school was fun, and life, simple.

Today, if you pick up the newspaper, you're likely to read something like this.

> The world is too big for us. Too much going on, too many crimes, too much violence and excitement. Try as you will you get behind in the race. . . . It's an incessant strain, to keep pace . . . and still, you lose ground. Science empties its discoveries on you so fast that you stagger beneath them in hopeless bewilderment. The political world is news seen so rapidly you're out of breath trying to keep pace with who's in and who's out. Everything is high pressure. Human nature can't endure much more![1]

Sounds like something out of this morning's paper, doesn't it? Actually, it appeared more than 150 years ago on June 16, 1833, in *The Atlantic Journal*—back in "the good old days."

And lest we think ours is the only generation to worry about an energy crisis, check out the headlines in the November 13, 1857, issue of the *Boston Globe:* "Energy Crisis Looms: World to Go Dark? Whale Blubber Scarce!"

In "the good old days" world wars raged, horses died from cholera in the streets of New York, and there was no indoor plumbing or air conditioning. So "the good old days" weren't all that good after all. And *this* day and time isn't all that bad—regardless of what the morning paper or the nightly news says.

Daniel assures us that although we may not know what the future holds, we do know *who* holds the future.

> "Let the name of God be blessed forever and ever,
> For wisdom and power belong to Him.
> And it is He who changes the times and the epochs;
> He removes kings and establishes kings;
> He gives wisdom to wise men,
> And knowledge to men of understanding." (Dan. 2:20–21)

1. Denis Waitley, *Seeds of Greatness* (Old Tappan, N.J.: Fleming H. Revell Co., 1983), p. 164.

Because God holds the future, we can rest in His sovereignty and echo David's words: "My times are in Thy hand" (Ps. 31:15a). In whatever generation, in whatever situation, our times are in God's hands.

I. My, How Times Have Changed

In a relatively few short years, our times have changed dramatically. World population, for example, did not reach one billion until 1850. But by 1930 that number doubled. And by 1960, the figure was three billion. Now we've arrived at five billion, and, by the year 2000, statisticians predict world population will rise to seven billion. And what about the changes in the book industry? Printed books became available in the 1500s with the invention of the printing press. By 1900, 35,000 books were printed. Today, more than 400,000 books are published annually. And this parallels our increase in knowledge. If we could measure it by height, all of man's knowledge from the beginning of time to 1845 would measure one inch. From 1845 to 1945 it would expand to three inches. From 1945 to today it would be the height of the Washington Monument. But don't worry, God knows everything that man has discovered. He understands nuclear energy and thermodynamics. He's not having a coronary over the speed of our world. Speaking of speed, that's another area that has undergone radical change. Horseback was the common mode of travel until 1800. Top speed? Twenty miles per hour. When the locomotive came along, we could travel up to 100 miles per hour. In 1952, the passenger jet reached 300 miles per hour. By 1979, planes jetted through the sky at twice that speed. Today, in space flight, astronauts can soar around the earth at more than 16,000 miles per hour. Denis Waitley, in *Seeds of Greatness,* forecasts what transportation could be like in the future. The possibilities are thrilling.

> In the year 2020, automobiles probably will be powered by an advanced battery pack for the short runs to and from offices and shopping. For the longer trips, cars will be powered by liquid-hydrogen engines. The exhaust from our future highway vehicles will be pure oxygen and steam, which are the by-products from burning liquid hydrogen. In effect, there will be tens of millions of rolling vacuum cleaners sucking the smog out of the cities and replacing it with air cleaner than the air above the Colorado Rockies. A big semitrailer will roar down the freeway, belching clouds of pure oxygen out of its stacks.[2]

Just as our world is growing and changing, so the church needs to be flexible in its approach. Times are different, and we need to adapt to the advancements of our age.

2. Waitley, *Seeds of Greatness,* p. 167.

II. But Some Things Never Change

In spite of the rapid rate of change in our world today, some things never change—like God. In Psalm 11, David no doubt feels threatened. His familiar shepherd life has been upended, and Saul is after him. Perhaps he is writing from the shelter of a cave. Looking around, he sees the cave as a metaphor of the rock-solid character of God.

> In the Lord I take refuge;
> How can you say to my soul, "Flee as a bird to your mountain;
> For, behold, the wicked bend the bow,
> They make ready their arrow upon the string,
> To shoot in darkness at the upright in heart.
> If the foundations are destroyed,
> What can the righteous do?" (vv. 1–3)

With the enemy forces all around and no way of escape, David needs a safe, solid foundation upon which to rest, one that's undisturbed and not subject to change. As his legs are wobbling amid unstable times, David is asking God the pointed question: "Lord, what can the righteous do when everything is up for grabs, when everything changes so much?" The answer to that question is found in 2 Timothy 2. With this letter, Paul says good-bye from a dungeon to his good friend and protégé, Timothy. This is Paul's final letter before his death, his last will and testament. In light of the changing times in which they live, he charges Timothy:

> Remind them of these things, and solemnly charge them in the presence of God not to wrangle about words, which is useless, and leads to the ruin of the hearers. (v. 14)

Word battles, Paul asserts, are not only useless, they're destructive. The Greek word for "ruin" is taken from the verb *katastrephō*. From it we get the word *catastrophe*. So Paul exhorts Timothy to stay off the verbal rabbit trails and stick to truths that are timeless.

> Be diligent to present yourself approved to God as a workman who does not need to be ashamed, handling accurately the word of truth. But avoid worldly and empty chatter, for it will lead to further ungodliness, and their talk will spread like gangrene. Among them are Hymenaeus and Philetus, men who have gone astray from the truth. . . . (vv. 15–18a)

Although false teachers are sending tremors through the church, Paul can solidly exhort Timothy on the basis that "the firm foundation of God stands" (v. 19a). That is the answer to David's question in Psalm 11:3. When everything is falling apart and quaking under your feet, the only stable ground is that which is laid by God. The Living Bible paraphrases it beautifully: "God's truth stands firm like a great rock, and nothing can shake it."[3] In that same verse, Paul implies that there is a twofold seal on that foundation.

> Nevertheless, the firm foundation of God stands, having this seal, "The Lord knows those who are His," and, "Let everyone who names the name of the Lord abstain from wickedness." (v. 19)

The first seal is invisible and secret: "The Lord knows those who are His." The second seal is visible and observed: "Let everyone who names the name of the Lord abstain from wickedness." Our challenge today is to stay up with the times to serve our generation. To do this, we must be willing to leave the familiar without disturbing the essential. We must serve both God and the present age.

Serving the Present Age

In the eighteenth century, Charles Wesley wrote this insightful, inspiring hymn.

> A charge to keep I have,
> A God to glorify,
> A never-dying soul to save,
> And fit it for the sky.
>
> To serve the present age,
> My calling to fulfill;
> O may it all my powers engage,
> To do my Master's will![4]

Serving the present age need not preclude serving God. Somehow, we have connected yesteryear's methodology with the message of Scripture, yesterday's technology with the Bible's timeless truth. In this computer age, many churches are still living in the Stone Age, scratching on rock tablets. How flexible are *you* in today's world? How contemporary is your approach to people? To programs? To problems?

An opposite extreme to living in the past is to trust in the future and in the people who will mold the future. Paul's picture of the days to come and those who will shape them is less than flattering.

> But realize this, that in the last days difficult times will come. For men will be lovers of self, lovers of money, boastful, arrogant, revilers, disobedient to parents, ungrateful, unholy, unloving, irreconcilable, malicious gossips, without self-control, brutal, haters of good,

3. The Living Bible (Wheaton, Ill.: Tyndale House Publishers, 1971).
4. Charles Wesley, "A Charge to Keep I Have."

> treacherous, reckless, conceited, lovers of pleasure rather than lovers of God. (2 Tim. 3:1–4)

Who can handle a future with savage people like that? Only those whose hearts are right with God and yielded to the controlling power of the Holy Spirit. The future will be difficult because there will be men opposed to the truth, "men of depraved mind" (v. 8).[5] Not only will men be depraved, but they will also be deceptive.

> But evil men and impostors will proceed from bad to worse, deceiving and being deceived. (v. 13)

This dark future raises an important question: How will the church survive the depravity and deception and difficulty?

III. The Essential Ingredient for Survival

The essential ingredient for survival is not isolation—it's *discernment.* Webster says that "discernment stresses skill and accuracy (as in reading character)."[6] It's the ability to spot error, to realize the Danger Ahead signs, to know the real issues, to distinguish truth from half-truth, pure motive from hidden agenda, and balance from fanaticism. To survive the future, you've got to have discernment. That's why Paul goes on to tell Timothy:

> You, however, continue in the things you have learned and become convinced of, knowing from whom you have learned them; and that from childhood you have known the sacred writings. (vv. 14–15a)

As we link ourselves with the foundational truth of God revealed in His Word, He'll give us all the discernment we need—to flex when necessary, and to stand firm when that is best.

How to Sharpen Your Discernment

Discernment is the skill of seeing the difference between what is good and what is bad (1 Kings 3:9).

It may be used on the assembly line to pick out flaws in manufacturing or in the college classroom to pick out flaws in philosophy or in choosing a business or marriage partner. Whatever its application, discernment becomes sharper when honed by the Scriptures.

> Thy commandments make me wiser than my
> enemies,
> For they are ever mine.
> I have more insight than all my teachers,
> For Thy testimonies are my meditation.

5. *Depraved* in the Greek is "corrupt in mind." The root term is "to corrupt," and the prefix with it means "down." Literally, it means "to corrupt down," as being corrupted to the depths.

6. *Webster's New Collegiate Dictionary,* see "discernment."

I understand more than the aged,
Because I have observed Thy precepts.
(Ps. 119:98–100)

How discerning are you when it comes to biblical truth and error? How sharp is your eye when it comes to spotting flaws in character? How skilled are you when it comes to discerning what is of eternal value in your daily schedule and what isn't?

If your spiritual vision is a little blurry, Scripture can be the corrective lenses that bring everything into focus.

IV. Suggestions for Maintaining Balance

Here are a couple of suggestions to help you and your church maintain a balance between stability and flexibility.

A. Changing times require the willingness to retool and flex when needed. Ask yourself: Is this style of ministry the best approach to use in light of the times in which we're living? Will it compromise Scripture to alter our style? How willing are we to flex?

B. Changeless truths require the discipline to resist and fight when necessary. No amount of futuristic technique and technology gives us the right to contradict the Bible or deny its truths. That's our refuge, our foundation. And it doesn't change whether the message is told by satellite to millions of people simultaneously . . . or proclaimed from a horse and buggy to a handful of people two centuries ago.

Living Insights

Study One

Do you believe we are in the last days? Every so often it's good to return to 2 Timothy 3 for a description of the last days to refresh our memory. Since one of the characteristics of that time is false teaching, let's study that area further.

- A helpful cross-reference to 2 Timothy 3 is 2 Peter 2. Read through the chapter and list the descriptions of the false teachers in the chart that follows. As you become familiar with these destructive qualities, remember Paul's admonition to Timothy: If you hold to the teachings of Scripture, God will give you the wisdom to discern the false from the true.

False Teachers in the Last Days—2 Peter 2	
Verses	Descriptions

Living Insights

Study Two

Even though times change, the Word of God remains timeless. Think about all the changes that have occurred in *your* lifetime. What a remarkable contrast to the security in the unchanging Word of God.

- Bring together your family or a group of close friends for a discussion. Talk about the changes that have occurred in your lifetime—in technology, science, communication, transportation, and so on. If you are a parent, your children will love this exercise! After you've discussed the changes, talk about the place God's Word has had in your life, even through all these changes.

Last-Days Lifestyle

2 Timothy 3:1–4:5

As a review of the previous lessons and to bring you back to basics, we'd like to give you this multiple-choice quiz. Ready? No fair peeking at the answers.

1. What is the primary purpose of the church?
   a. to be a lighthouse in the community
   b. to glorify God
   c. to help the hungry and hurting
   d. to give teenagers a place to go on Saturday night

2. We suggested the acronym *WIFE* for our objectives as a church. *W* represents worship; *F,* fellowship; *E,* evangelism. What does the *I* represent?
   a. image
   b. involvement
   c. instruction
   d. indebtedness

3. Next we talked about "A Church with a Contagious Style." The first letters of the four attributes of a contagious church spell the word *GRAB. G,* we are to be gracious; *R,* relevant; *A,* authentic. What does *B* represent?
   a. big
   b. biblical
   c. buildings
   d. boring

4. We then pointed out the difference between a metropolitan church and a neighborhood church. One aspect we covered was delegation. In a smaller church, the senior pastor can be in the middle of everything and often is. But in a larger church, a lot of responsibility has to be delegated. When we looked in the Old Testament, we found one person confronting another person with the importance of delegation. Who were these two people?
   a. Samson and Delilah
   b. Jonathan and David
   c. Sarah and Abraham
   d. Jethro and Moses

5. Finally, we talked about how some things must change to stay up with the times, but other things must remain as they have always been. We looked at 2 Timothy 2:19 and found a promise written by Paul to

Timothy: "Nevertheless, *this* stands firm. Don't worry about its ever being destroyed." What will never be destroyed?

a. the doxology
b. the foundation
c. our method of evangelism
d. the placement of the announcements in the church service

OK, it's time to grade. First: the primary purpose of the church is (b), to glorify God. That is at the root of everything we do. Second: you're correct if you put (c), instruction. Third: our style is to be gracious, relevant, authentic, and (b), biblical. Fourth: the answer is (d). It was Jethro who confronted his son-in-law, Moses, and encouraged him to delegate many of his responsibilities. And fifth: the answer is (b), the foundation of God never changes.

No matter how you answered those questions, there's one question we would all answer the same: Would you say that times are worse today, spiritually, than they have ever been? Probably 100 percent of us would say, "Without a doubt." There is no question that our spiritual and moral values are worse today than they have ever been.

I. General Evaluation: What We Should Expect

We must burst the balloon of the blind optimist who keeps thinking things will get better and better. Jesus Himself taught in Matthew 24 that they would only worsen.

> As He was sitting on the Mount of Olives, the disciples came to Him privately, saying, "Tell us, when will these things be, and what will be the sign of Your coming, and of the end of the age?" And Jesus answered and said to them, "See to it that no one misleads you. For many will come in My name, saying, 'I am the Christ,' and will mislead many. And you will be hearing of wars and rumors of wars; see that you are not frightened, for those things must take place, but that is not yet the end. For nation will rise against nation, and kingdom against kingdom, and in various places there will be famines and earthquakes. But all these things are merely the beginning of birth pangs. Then they will deliver you to tribulation, and will kill you, and you will be hated by all nations on account of My name. And at that time many will fall away and will deliver up one another and hate one another. And many false prophets will arise, and will mislead many. And because lawlessness is increased, most people's love will grow cold." (vv. 3–12)

Jesus informs us of a crescendo of wickedness—conditions will worsen, homes will weaken, and morals will wane.

A. **Conditions will worsen.** International conflicts will only grow and abound, increasing to such a measure that nations will no longer be able to tolerate each other. They will become irreconcilable, refusing to even negotiate. Disease will escalate; the crime rate will soar. In short, the world will be in upheaval.

B. **Homes will weaken.** There isn't a person today who doesn't know of a family touched by divorce. In fact, some of you would even admit, "I never wanted it, and it hit me. I am its victim. My family is weakened. Our relationships are fractured. The very thing years ago that I swore would not happen to this home *has* happened. And it's taken its toll on my children, and it will on my grandchildren too."

C. **Morals will wane.** What once made us blush, we now watch with ease on the television set. Back in 1939, a simple four-letter word made front-page headlines when it was used in the film *Gone with the Wind.* Now much worse is commonly heard in films, TV, and everyday language. It's easy to think things are way out of hand, that we've lost control, that God must be wringing His hands, wondering, What will I do with this world? But that is not the case, according to 2 Timothy 2:19.

> Nevertheless, the firm foundation of God stands, having this seal, "The Lord knows those who are His," and, "Let everyone who names the name of the Lord abstain from wickedness."

Questions to Consider

The whole issue of the end times raises some important questions, not just prophetically, but personally. The question is not, Will things be difficult, or Is God in control? Instead we must ask ourselves: How do I minister? How do I live? How do I relate in a world that has lost its way? What can my church do to make a dent? What's the best way to minister in a world that's speeding in the wrong direction? Should we build our walls thicker and higher and have keys that we distribute only to our own so that we have a safe little pocket of purity and protection? What do we do? How do we survive?

II. Spiritual Instruction: How We Must Respond

In chapter 3 of 2 Timothy, we come to one of the most vivid accounts of wickedness in all the Bible.

> But realize this, that in the last days difficult times will come. (v. 1)

A. Brief analysis of "difficult times." In Timothy's day, Paul was imprisoned, Christians were being martyred daily, and if you made your faith known, you were marked by the government. So why does Paul tell Timothy to realize something that is already abundantly clear? Remember that young pastor? He had a temperament that needed to be stirred up (see 2 Tim. 1:6). Maybe he thought, "Well, opposition is bad right now, but this won't be permanent. The storm will blow over, and later on things will get better." Anticipating that response, Paul says, "Realize this, Timothy, this last-days lifestyle is here to stay." Look again at the words: "Difficult times will come." *Difficult* comes from a Greek word that means "hard, harsh, hard to deal with." The King James Version renders it "perilous times." It's used in Matthew 8:28 to describe the appearance and actions of two men who had demons. And the translation there is "exceedingly violent." The last times will be savage. There will be fewer people who really want to walk with God . . . fewer mates to share an equal yoke with. It will be harder and harder to rear a family that takes God seriously. And the picture only gets worse.

> For men will be lovers of self, lovers of money, boastful, arrogant, revilers, disobedient to parents, ungrateful, unholy, unloving, irreconcilable, malicious gossips, without self-control, brutal, haters of good, treacherous, reckless, conceited, lovers of pleasure rather than lovers of God; holding to a form of godliness, although they have denied its power; and avoid such men as these. For among them are those who enter into households and captivate weak women weighed down with sins, led on by various impulses, always learning and never able to come to the knowledge of the truth. And just as Jannes and Jambres opposed Moses,[1] so these men also oppose the truth, men of depraved mind, rejected as regards the faith. (2 Tim. 3:2–8)

Depravity and corruption will fill people's minds, and they will reject their faith. They will be counterfeit—tried and found wanting. But lest Timothy become too distressed, Paul gives the young pastor a ray of hope in verse 9.

> But they will not make further progress; for their folly will be obvious to all, as also that of those two [Jannes and Jambres] came to be.

1. These were two magicians in Pharaoh's court who attempted to counterfeit God's power. As Moses performed miracles through God's power, Jannes and Jambres did theirs through the power of Satan.

Fortunately, there will still be those in the church who will be able to discern truth from error. In *Guard the Gospel,* a very practical book on 2 Timothy, John Stott writes this paragraph.

> We sometimes get distressed in our day—rightly and understandably—by the false teachers who oppose the truth and trouble the church, especially by the sly and slippery methods of backdoor religious traders. But we need have no fear, even if a few weak people may be taken in, even if falsehood becomes fashionable. For there is something patently spurious about heresy, and something self-evidently true about the truth. Error may spread and be popular for a time. But it 'will not get very far'. In the end it is bound to be exposed, and the truth is sure to be vindicated. This is a clear lesson of church history. Numerous heresies have arisen, and some have seemed likely to triumph. But today they are largely of antiquarian interest. God has preserved his truth in the church.[2]

B. Wise answers to all who minister. Now with that little bit of hope, the apostle turns his attention to the man receiving the letter and, indirectly, to all of us living in the last-days era. In doing so, he gives us some wise answers on how not only to survive the era in which we live but to abound.

1. **Follow the model of the faithful.** In verses 10–12, Paul urges Timothy that even though times are difficult, he must distinguish himself from the crowd.

> But you followed my teaching, conduct, purpose, faith, patience, love, perseverance, persecutions, and sufferings, such as happened to me at Antioch, at Iconium and at Lystra; what persecutions I endured, and out of them all the Lord delivered me! And indeed, all who desire to live godly in Christ Jesus will be persecuted.

Last-Days Lifestyle

After Paul's conversion on the Damascus Road (Acts 9), he lived his life for Jesus. His life served not only as an example for Timothy to emulate, but it lives on in the pages of Scripture as an example for us. He wasn't perfect, and we shouldn't put him on the same pedestal as Christ. But he did live a life worth following. Paul himself said that we "offer ourselves as a

2. John R. W. Stott, *Guard the Gospel* (Downers Grove, Ill.: InterVarsity Press, 1973), p. 91.

model for you, that you might follow our example" (2 Thess. 3:9).

Whose footsteps are you following? Who is your model? Whoever it is, make sure that person is following in the footsteps of the Savior and leading you closer to Him (see 1 Cor. 11:1).

The word *follow* is the same term Luke uses in his Gospel. As a historian and practicing physician, he investigated all the facts before he wrote about the life of Christ. So when Luke followed Christ, it wasn't from a distance. He got as close as he possibly could to pick up the qualities that marked His life.

2. **Return to the truth of the past.** How do you make it in a difficult era—like the one described in 2 Timothy 3:13?

> Evil men and imposters will proceed from bad to worse, deceiving and being deceived.

Paul gives the answer in verses 14–15: by returning to the truth of your past. In doing so, he assures Timothy that he's set apart from these apostates.

> You, however, continue in the things you have learned and become convinced of, knowing from whom you have learned them; and that from childhood you have known the sacred writings which are able to give you the wisdom that leads to salvation through faith which is in Christ Jesus.

Returning to Your Roots

If you go back to 2 Timothy 1:5, you will see that Timothy's sincere faith first resided in his grandmother Lois and his mother, Eunice. Nothing is said of his father, but no doubt he was Greek in heritage and philosophy. Possibly, his father was unsaved. But Timothy's mother and his maternal grandmother are the ones who shaped his thinking. His faith became sincere at their knees, under their tutelage.

It's not only important what you learn, it's also important from *whom* you learn. For Timothy it was his mother and grandmother. Who is it with you? Were you blessed with parents who loved God? Were you blessed with grandparents who did? Perhaps neighbors or friends?

Return to the truth of your past. Review those lives and events that led you to Christ. Remember them, renew them, rely on them. And when hard times come and almost level you, go back to your roots. There you'll find security.

Living Insights

Study One

Second Timothy 3 is a graphic presentation of the last-days lifestyle. Let's examine this chapter more thoroughly and, in doing so, increase our understanding of these last days.

- With 2 Timothy 3 in front of you, let's return to the method of paraphrasing. Write out this chapter in your own words. Again, this will help you derive greater meaning from the text. If paraphrasing the entire chapter seems a little ambitious, bite off a more manageable portion.

2 Timothy 3

Living Insights

Study Two

What kind of people will make a positive impact on the kind of world described in 2 Timothy 3? People who live in *contrast* to the world, who possess *commitment* to the task in front of them, and who are *consistent* with the message they proclaim.

- Let's do a little self-evaluation in these three areas. Rate yourself, with 1 being lowest and 5, highest; and explain your answer in the space provided.

  Contrast to the World 1 2 3 4 5

  Why? ____

  ____

  ____

  Commitment to the Task 1 2 3 4 5

  Why? ____

  ____

  ____

  Consistent with the Message 1 2 3 4 5

  Why? ____

  ____

  ____

Stayin' Ready for Quittin' Time

2 Timothy 3:10–4:5

When you work in a factory, your life is regulated by a whistle. The shrill signal punctuates your day—when you punch in, when it's time for lunch, and when it's quittin' time.

Some people have worked in a factory for so many years that they hardly need to hear the whistle. Instinctively, they know when it's time to get off work. In fact, most are ready to punch out and leave by the time the whistle blows. They don't need to *start* getting ready for quittin' time because they *stay* ready for quittin' time!

The Scriptures tell us to be on the alert for the final "quittin' time." But when our Lord's coming is announced, it won't be with a whistle.

> For the Lord Himself will descend from heaven with a shout,[1] with the voice of the archangel,[2] and with the trumpet of God; and the dead in Christ shall rise first. Then we who are alive and remain shall be caught up together with them in the clouds to meet the Lord in the air. (1 Thess. 4:16–17a)

Are you staying ready for "quittin' time"? Does it ever dawn on you that it may happen today? The thought may never have crossed your mind until just now, but the Lord repeatedly emphasized the imminency of His return.

I. A Few Predictions from Jesus' Life

Let's look at one passage from each of the Gospels to see just how widespread these predictions were.

A. Matthew 24. Verses 42–44 harbinger His return.

> "Therefore be on the alert, for you do not know which day your Lord is coming. But be sure of this, that if the head of the house had known at what time of the night the thief was coming, he would have been on the alert and would not have allowed his house to be broken into. For this reason you be ready too; for the Son of Man is coming at an hour when you do not think He will."

If you have ever had your home or business invaded by a thief, you know that the thief succeeded because he entered by surprise. In using that analogy, Jesus is saying that He will come when you least expect Him.

1. The word means "an outcry."

2. Scripture tells us on more than one occasion that the angelic voices are loud shouts or like the sound of thunder rolling across the mountainside (see Rev. 5:2, 10:1–4).

B. Mark 13. In a parallel passage, Jesus says,

> "Take heed, keep on the alert; for you do not know when the appointed time is. It is like a man, away on a journey, who upon leaving his house and putting his slaves in charge, assigning to each one his task, also commanded the doorkeeper to stay on the alert. Therefore, be on the alert—for you do not know when the master of the house is coming, whether in the evening, at midnight, at cockcrowing, or in the morning—lest he come suddenly and find you asleep." (vv. 33–36)

The Roman night was divided into four watches, three hours each. The first watch was from six to nine at night. The second watch was from nine until midnight. The third watch was from midnight until three, known as the *gallicinium,* a familiar Latin term that means "cockcrowing." It probably was derived from the early rising rooster that would stretch his neck and sound the first cry to usher in the morning. The fourth watch was from three until six.

C. Luke 21. Christ's warning in Luke is similar to those in the other synoptic Gospels, but here He employs an entirely different image to communicate His message.

> "Be on guard, that your hearts may not be weighted down with dissipation and drunkenness and the worries of life, and that day come on you suddenly like a trap; for it will come upon all those who dwell on the face of all the earth. But keep on the alert at all times, praying in order that you may have strength to escape all these things that are about to take place, and to stand before the Son of Man." (vv. 34–36)

Christ's coming will not only be surprising, like a thief; it will be sudden, like a trap springing to ensnare its unaware victim. This means we should not let anything dull the edge of our alertness, whether wine or the worries of life.

D. John 14 and 16. In John 14, Jesus is with His disciples on the night before His arrest. The disciples were expecting Jesus to establish His kingdom on earth, so when He told them of His imminent death, they were taken off guard.

> "Let not your heart be troubled; believe in God, believe also in Me. In My Father's house are many dwelling places;[3] if it were not so, I would have told you;

3. The King James Version translates this word "mansions," painting a misleading picture of an opulent hillside mansion on a sprawling estate. The idea is really more of "apartments." The appealing thing about heaven is not its lavish beauty, but rather being with Jesus, one you love and who loves you.

> for I go to prepare a place for you. And if I go and prepare a place for you, I will come again, and receive you to Myself; that where I am, there you may be also." (vv. 1–3)

The promise of a prepared place is not based upon our alertness or our obedience—it's unconditional. But what can we expect in the meantime, while we're waiting? Jesus answers that question for us in the last verse of chapter 16.

> "These things I have spoken to you, that in Me you may have peace. In the world you have tribulation, but take courage; I have overcome the world." (v. 33)

Sometimes life will be difficult. But we can live courageously, knowing that He has overcome the world.

II. Specific Principles from Paul's Pen

Turning from the last days of Christ to the last days of Paul, we span a period of about thirty years. In 2 Timothy, Paul's last letter before he died, the apostle gives Timothy four principles.

A. Follow the model of the faithful. After describing the morally turbulent times in which he lived, Paul instructed Timothy to be different from the decaying world around him.

> But you followed my teaching, conduct, purpose, faith, patience, love, perseverance, persecutions, and sufferings, such as happened to me at Antioch, at Iconium and at Lystra; what persecutions I endured, and out of them all the Lord delivered me! And indeed, all who desire to live godly in Christ Jesus will be persecuted. (3:10–12)

We all live by following someone else's example. Paul encourages us to follow the example of the faithful. Watch them. Learn from them. Emulate them.

B. Return to the truth of your past. In a moral drought, a return to your roots can help you survive, just as it did Timothy.

> But evil men and impostors will proceed from bad to worse, deceiving and being deceived. You, however, continue in the things you have learned and become convinced of, knowing from whom you have learned them; and that from childhood you have known the sacred writings which are able to give you the wisdom that leads to salvation through faith which is in Christ Jesus. (vv. 13–15)

Timothy's roots were healthy and strong, reaching back two generations. Because of this heritage, he could draw upon very rich, fertile memories and find the courage to go on. The truth in these "sacred writings" (2 Tim. 3:15) that was imparted by his mother and grandmother not only educated Timothy but equipped him for life. Paul notes parenthetically in verses 16–17 that these sacred writings are profitable, both for creed and for conduct.

> All Scripture is inspired[4] by God and profitable for teaching, for reproof, for correction, for training in righteousness; that the man of God may be adequate, equipped for every good work.

Paul tells Timothy that all of this has been deposited into his reservoir, and he encourages him to draw upon those Scriptures when times are hard.

C. Proclaim the message of Christ. In chapter 4, verses 1–2, Paul gives Timothy a strong admonition.

> I solemnly charge you in the presence of God and of Christ Jesus, who is to judge the living and the dead, and by His appearing and His kingdom: preach the word; be ready in season and out of season; reprove, rebuke, exhort, with great patience and instruction.

Two things stand out in this passage: urgency and consistency. *Get ready and stay ready*—that's the thrust of Paul's charge to Timothy. Whether it's convenient or inconvenient, whether you feel good or bad, whether you're in public or in private. There is a beautiful simplicity about this passage. Paul tells Timothy to "preach the word." Not some sophisticated philosophy. Not theories or complex opinions. Just the word—God's Word.

A Simple Lesson from History

One of the many stories that survived the Civil War is about a letter that took only three lines. Yet its simple message changed the course of history and led to the end of the war. It is addressed to Lieutenant General Grant. It is dated April 7, 1865, 11:00 A.M. It is signed simply, "A. Lincoln."

The three lines read:

> General Sheridan says "If the thing is pressed I think that Lee will surrender." Let the thing be pressed.[5]

The thing was pressed, and the bloodiest war in all our history ended. Two days later, at Appomattox courthouse, Robert E. Lee surrendered.

4. This is the classic passage on the inspiration of Scripture. The word "inspired" is *theopneustos.* It is a compound word from *theos* and *pneuma,* literally meaning "God-breathed."

5. Carl Sandburg, *Abraham Lincoln: The War Years* (New York, N.Y.: Harcourt, Brace and Co., 1939), vol. 4, p. 185.

> Let the thing be pressed, and you'll find victory. Take the Bible for what it says. Apply it where you live, and it will work. When the bottom drops out of your life, the Bible works. When the one you love walks away, the Bible works. When the barrier is absolutely beyond measuring and you can't see your way through, let the thing be pressed—because the Bible, in its powerful simplicity, works!

D. Maintain an exemplary life. Verses 3–5 provide us with this last principle.

> For the time will come when they will not endure sound doctrine; but wanting to have their ears tickled, they will accumulate for themselves teachers in accordance to their own desires; and will turn away their ears from the truth, and will turn aside to myths. But you, be sober in all things, endure hardship, do the work of an evangelist, fulfill your ministry.

There are four staccato commands in verse 5.

1. **"Be sober in all things."** Because people are unstable, forever on a search for the fad and the clever, make sure that *you* stay calm and steady. Look for the ministry that nurtures those qualities. Stay away from the ones that merely follow the latest trends.
2. **"Endure hardship."** Although most want what is best for them, they will resent and resist the hard times—but make sure that *you* stay at the hard task of enduring.
3. **"Do the work of an evangelist."** Since more and more people will be living their lives apart from the knowledge of Christ, make sure that *you* keep presenting it.
4. **"Fulfill your ministry."** Realizing that the phony and the false will be on the increase, make sure that *you* tell and live the truth.

III. Timeless Facts That Maintain Our Readiness

How can we stay ready for "quittin' time"? How can we guarantee that we won't be surprised at the shout, the voice, and the trumpet from heaven? Verses 6–8 give us the answer.

A. Consider your life an offering to God—following the example of Paul—rather than a monument to man.

> For I am already being poured out as a drink offering. (v. 6a)

B. Remember that finishing well is the final proof that the truth works.

> I have fought the good fight, I have finished the course, I have kept the faith. (v. 7)

The truth is what draws you to the finish line.

C. Fix your eyes on the rewards of heaven rather than the allurements of earth.

> In the future there is laid up for me the crown of righteousness, which the Lord, the righteous Judge, will award to me on that day; and not only to me, but also to all who have loved His appearing. (v. 8)

So much of life depends on focus, doesn't it? We need eyes not only to see *with*, but to see *through*. A prime illustration of this is in Genesis 13, where we find Abraham and his nephew Lot living on the same property. Abraham had generously given Lot some of his cattle, but before long, their respective herds multiplied so much that the land couldn't sustain them all. Abraham graciously allowed Lot the choice of land on which to pasture his cattle.

> And Lot lifted up his eyes and saw all the valley of the Jordan, that it was well watered everywhere. (v. 10a)

Lot saw how beautiful and lush the land was—but he didn't see *through* it. He didn't stop to think about the perversion in Sodom and Gomorrah and how that might affect him and his family. To survive difficult times, you need eyes to see through, not just with.

Eyes Set on Eternity

William Blake wrote in a poem:

> This life's dim windows of the soul
> Distort the heavens from pole to pole
> And lead you to believe a lie
> When you see with, not through, the eye.[6]

If we, as God's people, hope to stay ready for "quittin' time," we'll need to follow the model of the faithful. We'll need to return to the truth of the past. We'll need to proclaim the message of Christ. We'll need to maintain an exemplary life. And we must keep our eyes open, not simply to see with, but to see through the dim windows of this earth into eternity (see Matt. 6:19–31).

6. Gordon MacDonald, *Restoring Your Spiritual Passion* (Nashville, Tenn.: Oliver-Nelson Books, 1986), p. 55.

Living Insights

Study One

There is no doubt that we are in the last days. No major prophetic events are left to be fulfilled before the Lord returns. Let's take a closer look at the words of Christ on this subject.

- We began this message with some words from Jesus on the topic of His return. Choose one of those passages from the list below and examine it in more detail. Record your observations in the space provided.

The Last Days

Matthew 24:42–44	Luke 21:34–36
Mark 13:33–36	John 14:1–3, 16:33

Living Insights

Study Two

Have you been staying ready for "quittin' time"? Are there areas of your life that need cleaning up? Let's give some attention to these issues through the avenue of prayer.

- Using the main points of this lesson as a guide, pray for the Lord's help in making you the kind of person that is truly ready for "quittin' time." Be honest in confessing your faults, admitting your needs, and asking for assistance. Make this a special time of tenderness between you and God.

The Hardest Part of Harvesting

Matthew 9:35–38

Seeing thousands of people streaming toward Him, eager to hear His teaching and see His miracles, Jesus said to His disciples, "The harvest is plentiful, but the workers are few" (Matt. 9:37).

The job of harvesting for God's kingdom is overwhelming. Those without Christ will always outnumber those with Christ. However, we can glean four principles from the Scriptures that will help us get the job done.

First, Scripture is clear that we need to share our faith.

> Faith comes from hearing, and hearing by the word of Christ. (Rom. 10:17)

No one receives Christ in a vacuum. A person comes to Christ by hearing the good news, either from a song, a sermon, or the printed page.

Second, we need to leave our familiar world—that safe circle of family and friends—and penetrate the world of those without Christ.

> "Whoever will call upon the name of the Lord will be saved." How then shall they call upon Him in whom they have not believed? And how shall they believe in Him whom they have not heard? And how shall they hear without a preacher? And how shall they preach unless they are sent? (vv. 13–15a)

Third, we need to invest our abilities and talents.

> Since we have gifts that differ according to the grace given to us, let each exercise them accordingly: if prophecy, according to the proportion of his faith; if service, in his serving; or he who teaches, in his teaching; or he who exhorts, in his exhortation; he who gives, with liberality; he who leads, with diligence; he who shows mercy, with cheerfulness. (12:6–8)[1]

Fourth, we need to give our money. The crop doesn't get harvested without laborers in the field. And laborers need to eat. Paul says that the one who works hard at preaching and teaching deserves to be supported by his work.

> For the Scripture says, "You shall not muzzle the ox while he is threshing," and "The laborer is worthy of his wages." (1 Tim. 5:18)

This message was not a part of the original series but is compatible with it.

1. Compare Matthew 25:14–30 and 1 Corinthians 3:10–15.

Yet, when it comes to harvesting the Lord's harvest, none of these principles is primary. What *is* primary can be seen in the uncommon approach to evangelism by Jesus.

I. Analysis of Jesus' Uncommon Approach

As we turn our attention to the ninth chapter of Matthew, we find that Jesus' approach to evangelism was one of compassion. He doesn't exhort His followers to share their faith or leave their surroundings or invest their talents or give their money. Beginning in verse 35, we'll follow Jesus as He ministered and observe what He does tell them.

> And Jesus was going about all the cities and the villages, teaching in their synagogues, and proclaiming the gospel of the kingdom, and healing every kind of disease and every kind of sickness. And seeing the multitudes, He felt compassion for them, because they were distressed and downcast like sheep without a shepherd. (vv. 35–36)

The two words *distressed* and *downcast* paint a bleak picture. The former means "harassed"; the latter, "thrown down," as thrown down to the floor or prostrate on the ground. William Barclay renders the word *distressed* as "bewildered" and writes in his commentary:

> The Jewish leaders, who should have been giving men strength to live, were bewildering men with subtle arguments about the Law, which had no help and comfort in them. When they should have been helping men to stand upright, they were bowing them down under the intolerable burden of the Scribal Law. They were offering men a religion which was a burden instead of a support. We must always remember that the Christian religion exists, not to discourage, but to encourage, not to weigh men down with burdens, but to lift them up with wings.[2]

Seeing these burdened people, Jesus was filled with *compassion.* The Greek word is *splagchna,* meaning "inward parts, entrails." The Greeks believed that deep within the bowels was the seat of the emotions, of violent passions, and of great affections. To have *splagchna* was to be moved deep down inside, to be gripped with compassion in a way that brought tears to the eyes. Up till now, Jesus had been the center of attention. *He* was the one who preached. *He* was the one who felt compassion. The disciples, meanwhile, were on the sidelines. But in verse 37, the emphasis shifts.

> Then He said to His disciples, "The harvest is plentiful, but the workers are few."

2. William Barclay, *The Gospel of Matthew,* 2d ed., The Daily Study Bible Series (Philadelphia, Pa.: Westminster Press, 1958), vol. 1, p. 365.

Abruptly, Jesus changed metaphors from sheep and shepherd to harvest and workers. In the sheep-and-shepherd metaphor, we see man's need met by God. In the harvest-and-workers metaphor, however, we see God's need met by man. To evangelize the world requires the involvement of people. But, although the vision to reach the world was passed by Christ to the disciples, the compassion, or *splagchna,* was not. In Matthew 14:14–17, we see an example of the difference in attitude, where Jesus' compassion is juxtaposed to the disciples' callousness.

> And when He went ashore, He saw a great multitude, and felt compassion for them, and healed their sick. And when it was evening, the disciples came to Him, saying, "The place is desolate, and the time is already past; so send the multitudes away, that they may go into the villages and buy food for themselves." But Jesus said to them, "They do not need to go away; you give them something to eat!" And they said to Him, "We have here only five loaves and two fish."

Notice again in 15:29–33 that the empathy of Jesus stands out in contrast to the indifference of the disciples.

> And departing from there, Jesus went along by the Sea of Galilee, and having gone up to the mountain, He was sitting there. And great multitudes came to Him, bringing with them those who were lame, crippled, blind, dumb, and many others, and they laid them down at His feet; and He healed them, so that the multitude marveled as they saw the dumb speaking, the crippled restored, and the lame walking, and the blind seeing; and they glorified the God of Israel. And Jesus called His disciples to Him, and said, "I feel compassion for the multitude, because they have remained with Me now three days and have nothing to eat; and I do not wish to send them away hungry, lest they faint on the way." And the disciples said to Him, "Where would we get so many loaves in a desolate place to satisfy such a great multitude?"

In 19:13–14, the disciples go so far as to actually rebuke the crowds. Again, Jesus' compassion outdistances their dullness of heart.

> Then some children were brought to Him so that He might lay His hands on them and pray; and the disciples rebuked them. But Jesus said, "Let the children alone, and do not hinder them from coming to Me; for the kingdom of heaven belongs to such as these."

Jesus meant for the gospel to extend to the ends of the earth. The disciples, however, had a much more exclusive view of their faith.

Returning to Matthew 9, we find Jesus giving the disciples an unusual assignment. He has just told them how big the harvest is, and we would expect Him to tell the disciples to start picking. Instead, He tells them to start praying.

> "Therefore beseech the Lord of the harvest to send out workers into His harvest." (v. 38)

The hardest part about evangelism is *praying*—praying with consistence . . . with compassion . . . with conviction . . . with confidence. But that is the model Jesus sets before us.

II. Results of Following Jesus' Model

Several results stem from prayer.

A. Transfer of compassion. When you pray for people, you begin to change. There is a transfer of *splagchna.* His ways become your ways; His will becomes your will. E. Stanley Jones writes:

> [Prayer is] surrender to the will of God and cooperation with that will. If I throw out a boathook from the boat and catch hold of the shore and pull, do I pull the shore to me, or do I pull myself to the shore? Prayer is not pulling God to my will, but the aligning of my will to the will of God.[3]

B. Shift in responsibility. Notice the shift in the very next verse.

> And having summoned His twelve disciples, He gave them authority over unclean spirits, to cast them out, and to heal every kind of disease and every kind of sickness. (10:1)

What happened between chapters 9 and 10? Twelve men got on their knees and prayed, that's what.

C. Active and personal involvement. We cannot continue to sit on the sidelines, watching while others work. We must get involved. Before, the disciples had only tagged along with Christ, content to stand in the shadows; but now, they were called to be an active part of the labor force. And they went out, two by two, preaching, casting out demons, and healing the sick (Mark 6:12–13).

D. Physical and mental exhaustion. After the disciples went out to preach the gospel, they returned to Christ to give Him their report.

> And the apostles gathered together with Jesus; and they reported to Him all that they had done and taught. (v. 30)

3. E. Stanley Jones, *A Song of Ascents: A Spiritual Autobiography* (Nashville, Tenn.: Abingdon Press, 1968), p. 383.

Realizing their physical and emotional batteries had run down, Jesus suggested a retreat for the weary laborers.

> And He said to them, "Come away by yourselves to a lonely place and rest a while." (For there were many people coming and going, and they did not even have time to eat.) And they went away in the boat to a lonely place by themselves. (vv. 31–32)

In the next chapter, Jesus instructed the disciples that that which defiles us comes from *within* (7:20–23). But there are also enemies from *without*—enemies that don't defile us necessarily, but nevertheless place a drain on us spiritually, emotionally, and physically: things like the needs of people, hurts, competition, manipulation, requests, expectations, arguments, questions, demands, hidden agendas, criticism. That's why the disciples needed to get away from the crowd . . . to receive spiritual, emotional, and physical nourishment so they could remain effective in their ministry.

The Cutting Edge

Some years ago a young man approached the foreman of a logging crew and asked for a job. "That depends," replied the foreman. "Let's see you fell this tree." The young man stepped forward and skillfully felled a great tree. Impressed, the foreman exclaimed, "Start Monday!"

Monday, Tuesday, Wednesday, Thursday rolled by, and Thursday afternoon the foreman approached the young man and said, "You can pick up your paycheck on the way out today."

Startled, he replied, "I thought you paid on Friday." "Normally we do," answered the foreman, "but we're letting you go today because you've fallen behind. Our daily felling charts show that you've dropped from first place on Monday to last on Wednesday."

"But I'm a hard worker," the young man objected. "I arrive first, leave last, and even have worked through my coffee breaks!"

The foreman, sensing the boy's integrity, thought for a minute and then asked, "Have you been sharpening your ax?"

The young man replied, *"I've been working too hard to take the time."*[4]

How about you? Have you been too busy, too hard at work to sharpen your ax? Prayer is the hone that gives you that sharp edge. Without it, the more work you do, the duller you'll get.

III. A Game Plan for Hard Work

Here's a strategy to help sharpen your prayer life. First, *connect prayer with something you already do every day.* It may be with an early morning cup of coffee or with a late night Bible reading. Second, *share this discipline with another person.* Be accountable to someone or some group. Third, *use some kind of tool that gives prayer wings.* It may be a picture on your desk or a scrapbook or a daily journal. Whatever it is, use it as a tool to prompt you to pray. Fourth, *record the answers as readily as you record your needs.* Fifth and finally, *look for ways to respond personally.* Get involved in the harvest. You can do more than pray *after* you have prayed, but you cannot do more than pray *until* you have prayed.

Living Insights

Study One

In lesson 10, the spotlight is taken off of the purpose, profile, and priorities of the church and placed on the pastor. But before we turn our attention there, let's review where we've been. Often it's in these times of looking back that our learning is underscored and affirmed.

- The list that follows gives the lesson titles in this series thus far. Page back through your Bible and this study guide and look for one important *truth* you gleaned from each lesson. Record your findings in the space provided.

The Church: Purpose, Profile, Priorities

The Taproot Purpose of Our Existence ______________________

____

____

Continued on next page

4. Anecdote by William D. Boyd, in *Liberating Ministry from the Success Syndrome,* by Kent and Barbara Hughes (Wheaton, Ill.: Tyndale House Publishers, 1987), p. 71.

The WIFE Every Church Should Marry ______________________

____

____

A Closer Look at Our WIFE ______________________________

____

____

A Church with a Contagious Style __________________________

____

____

Analysis of a Metropolitan Ministry ________________________

____

____

Changing Times—Changeless Truths _______________________

____

____

Last-Days Lifestyle ____________________________________

____

____

Stayin' Ready for Quittin' Time ___________________________

____

____

The Hardest Part of Harvesting ___________________________

____

____

Living Insights

Study Two

We looked at important truths from this series in Study One. Our focus in Study Two is on application, so let's redirect our review to that very important aspect.

- Return to your Bible and the lessons, this time looking for one helpful *application* you were able to make in each study. Write your applications in the space following each title.

The Church: Purpose, Profile, Priorities

The Taproot Purpose of Our Existence ______________________

____

____

The WIFE Every Church Should Marry ______________________

____

____

A Closer Look at Our WIFE ______________________

____

____

A Church with a Contagious Style ______________________

____

____

Analysis of a Metropolitan Ministry ______________________

____

____

Changing Times—Changeless Truths ______________________

____

____

Continued on next page

Last-Days Lifestyle ______________________________

____

____

Stayin' Ready for Quittin' Time ______________________________

____

____

The Hardest Part of Harvesting ______________________________

____

____

No Substitute for Integrity

Dr. Evan O'Neill Kane, a pioneer in the medical profession, was chief surgeon of New York City's Kane Summit Hospital.

During his thirty-seven years of experience, Dr. Kane had seen too many deaths and disabilities caused by general anesthesia. So, it was his studied opinion that most major operations could and should be done under the safer, local anesthesia.

His only problem was—he couldn't find any volunteers. Until one day . . . someone finally stepped forward to put his theory to the test.

In thirty-seven years, Dr. Evan Kane had conducted nearly four thousand appendectomies, all fairly routine. But this one would be different: the patient would remain awake throughout the entire operation.

Before surgery, the patient was prepped and wheeled into the operating room, where a local anesthesia was administered. Dr. Kane began the operation and carefully cut through the surface tissues, clamping off blood vessels en route to the appendix. Locating the organ, the sixty-year-old surgeon adroitly pulled it up and performed the surgery. The operation concluded successfully, with the patient experiencing only minor discomfort. In fact, the patient recovered with such remarkable speed that just two days after his surgery he was released from the hospital.

Dr. Kane's test was a brilliant success. The risks of general anesthesia *could* be avoided by using local anesthesia instead.

This milestone surgery was performed on February 15 . . . 1921. And you might want to note this final interesting fact: Dr. Evan O'Neill Kane and the patient who volunteered for the experimental procedure had a great deal in common—they were the same man![1]

For the remainder of this lesson, we want you to operate on yourself. It will be painful, but unless we are willing to undergo this type of self-surgery, we'll never stop the epidemic absence of integrity sweeping the world today.

I. No Substitute for Integrity

There is no such thing as *almost* having integrity. That's like almost being married. Either you are or you aren't. Unfortunately, as we look around us, we see many people who lack integrity.

This message was not a part of the original series but is compatible with it.

1. Based on *More of Paul Harvey's The Rest of the Story,* by Paul Aurandt (New York, N.Y.: William Morrow and Co., 1980), pp. 111–12.

A. **Shuttle disaster.** The date was January 28, 1986. It was a cold morning at Cape Canaveral, the Florida launch site of the *Challenger* space shuttle. Unbeknownst to the rest of the world, a war of words was waging between cautious engineers and bureaucratic executives. The engineers said no to the launch. The executives said yes. The executive decision ruled, and seventy seconds later seven people died. For an hour, the debris from that explosion rained down into the Atlantic. What went wrong? There was a breakdown in integrity—not only in the seal that held the fuel but in the individuals who made the decision to ignore the danger.

B. **Shiftless driving.** Less dramatic, but more widespread, is the slaughter of thousands on our highways each year. One-half of the deaths in automobile accidents are caused by alcohol and substance abuse—a breakdown of integrity.

C. **Spreading disease.** AIDS. Acquired Immune Deficiency Syndrome. The moral lapse in integrity that accounts for casual sex will someday blight our nation. According to the U.S. Surgeon General, by 1991 there will be 179,000 deaths from the disease in the U.S. alone.

D. **Stolen documents.** The military once bragged about its integrity. The marines bragged about their motto, *semper fidelis*—"always faithful." But the damage done by a few U.S. Marines who traded secrets to the Soviets for sex was incalculable. Clearly, an erosion of integrity.[2]

II. The Definition of Integrity

The Hebrew root of *integrity* means "whole, sound, unimpaired, entire."[3] It is the absence of double standards, deceit, and hypocrisy. Integrity includes being financially accountable and personally reliable. When under persecution, David used the word in Psalm 7:8.

> Vindicate me, O Lord, according to my... integrity.

When tempted, he said,

> Guard my soul and deliver me;
> Do not let me be ashamed, for I take refuge in Thee.
> Let integrity and uprightness preserve me,
> For I wait for Thee. (Ps. 25:20–21)

When chosen to serve, he responded.

> [God] also chose David His servant,
> And took him from the sheepfolds;

2. The information in points A–D is based on *Integrity,* by Ted W. Engstrom with Robert C. Larson (Waco, Tex.: Word Books, 1987), pp. 3–9.

3. The Hebrew word is *tom.*

From the care of the ewes with suckling lambs He brought him,
To shepherd Jacob His people,
And Israel His inheritance.
So he shepherded them according to the integrity of his heart,
And guided them with his skillful hands. (Ps. 78:70–72)

Even when elevated from the fields to the palace, David didn't let it go to his head. He kept his integrity and passed it on to his son. As Solomon said in Proverbs 20:7,

A righteous man who walks in his integrity—
How blessed are his sons after him.

Nothing is more permanent or obvious than the thumbprint of integrity—or the lack of it—that we leave on our children's lives.

Keeping Promises

Ted Engstrom gives a succinct definition of integrity:

> Simply put, *Integrity* is doing what you said you would do.[4]

It means you keep your promises.

When you promised to be faithful to your mate, integrity says you'll stay with that person no matter what—for better or for worse, for richer or for poorer, in sickness and in health.

If you promised the Lord that you would give Him the glory, integrity means you keep on doing that whether you're reduced to nothing or exalted to the highest pinnacle on earth.

If you promised a friend that you would return a call, integrity means you return it.

If you promised your child that you would spend Saturday together, integrity means you keep that appointment.

A promise is a holy thing, whether made to a chairman of the board—or to a child.

III. Examples of Integrity

You probably remember being thrilled as a little child with the heroic characters in the Bible. And why were you attracted to these stories? Because they were stories of integrity. See if these names don't stir your spirit.

A. Joseph. Mistreated and brutalized by his brothers, Joseph had the integrity of heart to look them in the eye years later and forgive them (Gen. 37–50, especially 45:1–7).

4. Engstrom with Larson, *Integrity,* p. 10.

B. Joshua. As Moses' successor, Joshua took the reins of leadership and showed integrity in his convictions. Before the vacillating nation of Israel, Joshua announced decisively: "Choose for yourselves today whom you will serve . . . but as for me and my house, we will serve the Lord" (Josh. 24:15).

C. David. Before David went out to fight Goliath, he looked the skeptical Saul right in the eye and said: "Who is this uncircumcised Philistine, that he should taunt the armies of the living God?" (1 Sam. 17:26b). Then, with the integrity of his convictions, he went out alone to face the taller, older, more experienced warrior.

D. Elijah. When Jezebel and Ahab killed the Lord's prophets and erected altars to worship Baal, Elijah confronted them with a daring challenge on Mount Carmel (1 Kings 18).

E. Paul and Silas. In Philippi, Paul and Silas were imprisoned. But even though they were alone in their jail cell and death was imminent, they maintained integrity in their faith by praying and singing hymns of praise to God (Acts 16:19–34).

F. Daniel. As Darius looked over the men he might appoint to rule over his kingdom, Daniel stood head and shoulders above the rest.

> It seemed good to Darius to appoint 120 satraps over the kingdom, that they should be in charge of the whole kingdom, and over them three commissioners (of whom Daniel was one), that these satraps might be accountable to them, and that the king might not suffer loss. Then this Daniel began distinguishing himself among the commissioners and satraps because he possessed an extraordinary spirit, and the king planned to appoint him over the entire kingdom. (Dan. 6:1–3)

What did Darius see in this older prophet? Integrity.

IV. The Tests of Integrity

Two major kinds of tests especially stress our integrity.

A. The test of adversity. When the bottom drops out, when the money doesn't come in, when our best dreams turn into our worst nightmares, we're faced with adversity. Solomon writes in Proverbs 24:10,

> If thou faint in the day of adversity, thy strength is small.[5] (KJV)

Even when we feel small, even when we feel like fainting, it's important to maintain our integrity.

5. See also Jeremiah 12:5.

B. The test of prosperity. The test of adversity simplifies life to the absolute basics—food, clothing, shelter. Success, however, is a much stiffer test. As adversity simplifies life, prosperity complicates it. When God reaches down and promotes you to a place of great authority, like he did with Daniel, your integrity will be tested. As soon as Daniel's peers heard he was going to be promoted, they began rifling through his files, spying on him, auditing him. They were determined to find something against him.

> But they could find no ground of accusation or evidence of corruption, inasmuch as he was faithful, and no negligence or corruption was to be found in him. (Dan. 6:4b)

That is integrity.

Integrity Check

If you are financially unaccountable, you are lacking in integrity. If you are unaccountable to someone, whether as an individual or as a church, your integrity is hanging by a thread.

Do you have anybody who is painfully honest with you? Do you have someone who asks you the hard questions about your spiritual life . . . your financial life . . . your sexual life?

If not, just remember, your integrity hangs by only a thin thread (compare Eccles. 4:12).

V. Some Summary Thoughts on Integrity

Several thoughts surface as we conclude our discussion on integrity.

A. True integrity implies you do what is right when no one is looking or when everyone is compromising. True integrity means you keep your promises, even when no one is there to check up on you or when everyone else is lying. Ministry is a character profession, and if a minister can't clean up his life, he should be out of the ministry. Martin Marty writes:

> After 1987, this Year of the Lie, where can people turn for truth? Philosophers remember old Diogenes, who still symbolizes the search because he went around truth-seeking with a lantern in broad daylight. . . .
>
> Some religious leaders do serve as models. . . . The hard times this year were for the religious prime-time characters. Some TV evangelists were unfaithful

> to their spouses and others doctored their autobiographies to cover past dissembling. The cynical public overlooks the model minister down the block and says to the celebrities, "Get your own act together and we might pay attention again."...
>
> The ancient Hebrews and the authors of the Greek New Testament spoke little about truth in the abstract, about truth in the impersonal sense. Instead they connected "truth" with the character of a faithful God and then wanted to see that quality reflected in humans.
>
> The biblical concept richer than "telling the truth" is expressed as "doing the truth." When someone "does" the truth, we can check that person out more readily than when talk about truth is only an intellectual game or tease....
>
> The liars and deceivers of recent exposure were so often loners, celebrities who had admirers and groupies but not friends who could be critical, who could keep honest....
>
> ...Character requires context. The French novelist Stendhal wrote that "One can acquire anything in solitude except character."[6]

B. Real integrity stays in place whether the test is adversity or prosperity. Whether you pass or fail, you must do it with integrity. Broken integrity means the spiritual leader forfeits the right to lead. In the Bible, men and women who once held highly visible roles in ministry and who compromised morally or ethically and were later forgiven never reached the same pinnacle or continued with the same success in their ministry.[7] A minister himself, A. W. Tozer wrote insightfully about the perils of the ministry.

> The ministry is one of the most perilous of professions....
>
> Satan knows that the downfall of a prophet of God is a strategic victory for him, so he rests not day or night devising hidden snares and deadfalls for the

6. Martin E. Marty, "Truth: Character in Context," *Los Angeles Times,* Sunday, Dec. 20, 1987, sec. 5, p. 1, col. 1.

7. Some say David is an exception to this. But if you study his life, after his affair with Bathsheba, David's reign goes downhill. He suffers defeat in the battlefield—something he never knew before. And he knows defeat at home—his daughter Tamar is raped, and his son Absalom leads a rebellion against him. In the final analysis, David never achieved the power he once knew.

ministry. Perhaps a better figure would be the poison dart that only paralyzes its victim, for I think that Satan has little interest in killing the preacher outright. An ineffective, half-alive minister is a better advertisement for hell than a good man dead. . . .

There are indeed some very real dangers of the grosser sort which the minister must guard against, such as love of money and women; but the deadliest perils are far more subtle than these. So let's concentrate on them.

There is, for one, the danger that the minister shall come to think of himself as belonging to a privileged class. Our "Christian" society tends to increase this danger by granting the clergy discounts and other courtesies. . . .

Another danger is that he may develop a perfunctory spirit in the performance of the work of the Lord. Familiarity may breed contempt even at the very altar of God. How frightful a thing it is for the preacher when he becomes accustomed to his work, when his sense of wonder departs, when he gets used to the unusual, when he loses his solemn fear in the presence of the High and Holy One; when, to put it bluntly, he gets a little bored with God and heavenly things. . . .

There is the danger also that the preacher may suffer alienation of spirit from the plain people. This arises from the nature of institutionalized Christianity. The minister meets religious people almost exclusively. People are on their guard when they are with him. They tend to talk over their own heads and to be for the time the kind of persons they think he wants them to be rather than the kind of persons they are in fact. This creates a world of unreality where no one is quite himself, but the preacher has lived in it so long that he accepts it as real and never knows the difference. . . .

Another peril that confronts the minister is that he may come unconsciously to love religious and philosophic ideas rather than saints and sinners. It is altogether possible to feel for the world of lost men the same kind of detached affection that the naturalist Fabre, say, felt for a hive of bees or a hill of black ants. They are something to study, to learn from, possibly even to help, but nothing to weep over or die for....

Another trap into which the preacher is in danger of falling is that he may do what comes naturally and just take it easy.... It is easy for the minister to be turned into a privileged idler, a social parasite with an open palm and an expectant look. He has no boss within sight; he is not often required to keep regular hours, so he can work out a comfortable pattern of life that permits him to loaf, putter, play, doze and run about at his pleasure. And many do just that.[8]

A Concluding Prayer for Integrity

God, give us men! A time like this demands
Strong minds, great hearts, true faith and ready
hands;
Men whom the lust of office does not kill;
Men whom the spoils of office cannot buy;
Men who possess opinions and a will;
Men who have honor; men who will not lie;
Men who can stand before a demagogue
And damn his treacherous flatteries without
winking!
Tall men, sun-crowned, who live above the fog
In public duty and in private thinking;
For while the rabble, with their thumb-worn
creeds,
Their large professions and their little deeds,
Mingle in selfish strife, lo! Freedom weeps,
Wrong rules the land and waiting Justice sleeps.[9]

8. A. W. Tozer, *God Tells the Man Who Cares* (Harrisburg, Pa.: Christian Publications, 1970), pp. 76–79.

9. Josiah Gilbert Holland, "God, Give Us Men!" from *The Best Loved Poems of the American People,* selected by Hazel Felleman (Garden City, N.Y.: Garden City Books, 1936), p. 132.

Living Insights

Study One

One of the finest accounts of a life filled with integrity is the story of Daniel. Have you looked at it lately? Let's take some time for a fresh look at this inspiring text.

- Read through Daniel 6, but this time use another version of the Bible. Those familiar phrases can take on new and fuller meanings if they are seen in a text that is brand new to you. Whether you choose a paraphrase or a translation, read slowly and carefully, allowing God to speak to you concerning Daniel's integrity. Drink it in!

Living Insights

Study Two

Being accountable to others is a great way to stay on target in every area of our lives. To maintain our integrity, we need to voluntarily submit ourselves to the scrutiny of others.

- Do you have a person to whom you are accountable? If you do, get together and discuss this issue of your integrity. Get into the hard issues, the tough questions. Make sure this person knows you thoroughly. If you don't have a friend like this, begin praying and searching for one. Accountability is essential if we are to be people of integrity.

Books for Probing Further

The church is not a building but a body. Sadly, many churches today have more the appearance of a vestigial organ than a vital organism. And their appendages for reaching out to a lost world look atrophied and arthritic compared to those of the New Testament church. To revitalize the church, we don't need new programs in the bulletin but a return to the age-old principles of the Bible. Paul gives us a body-building formula for health in Ephesians 4:15–16:

> Speaking the truth in love, we are to grow up in all aspects into Him, who is the head, even Christ, from whom the whole body, being fitted and held together by that which every joint supplies, according to the proper working of each individual part, causes the growth of the body for the building up of itself in love.

In this study guide we looked at the purpose, profile, and priorities of the church. Then we turned the magnifying glass away from the parish and onto the pastor to see the importance of integrity in living out our faith before the eyes of a watching world.

Now we want to conclude by providing you with some resources that will be helpful in building the kind of church that is a light to the world, a city set on a hill (Matt. 5:14).

Remember, just as a building is only as strong as its individual bricks, so the body is only as healthy as its individual members. And that puts a tremendous responsibility on you—to grow.

But growth is not mysterious or magic. We grow spiritually in much the same way we grow physically. So, eat right (1 Pet. 2:2), get enough spiritual exercise (Heb. 12:1), and make sure to get the rest you need (Matt. 11:28).

I. Purpose

Coleman, Robert E. *The Master Plan of Discipleship.* Old Tappan, N.J.: Fleming H. Revell Co., 1987. In this work, Dr. Robert Coleman examines the book of Acts to derive principles about church growth through evangelism and discipleship. He reveals that while specific procedures change, the basic pattern of the Great Commission has remained the same since the apostolic age.

———. *The Master Plan of Evangelism.* Old Tappan, N.J.: Fleming H. Revell Co., 1964. Here Coleman presents concepts for evangelism based on Christ's work with His disciples. These give us a clear objective of the Master's plan as well as a perfect example to follow.

Peterson, Eugene H. *A Long Obedience in the Same Direction.* Downers Grove, Ill.: InterVarsity Press, 1980. Peterson uses Psalms 120–130 to encourage the Christian pilgrim for the journey of faith. He focuses a chapter on each psalm and expounds its theme, which may center on service, worship, joy, work, happiness, humility, community, or blessing. Peterson shares with fellow travelers his warm, mature reflections from these psalms of faith.

II. Profile

Schaeffer, Francis A. *The Church at the End of the Twentieth Century.* Downers Grove, Ill.: Inter-Varsity Press, 1970. Dr. Schaeffer analyzes the contemporary church and the many pressures exerted upon it. He sets forth biblical guidelines for a truly Christian community and presents a program for individual and institutional reform.

———. *The Church before the Watching World.* Downers Grove, Ill.: Inter-Varsity Press, 1971. This book begins with a historical critique of theological liberalism. Then it examines the present purity of the church. It concludes with a set of principles to govern the attitudes and actions of Christians so they can stand before the watching world as a city set upon a hill.

Stott, John. *One People.* Expanded and updated. Old Tappan, N.J.: Fleming H. Revell Co., 1982. This popular study of the true biblical roles for leaders and laypeople helps churches become caring communities.

III. Priorities

Peterson, Eugene H. *Earth and Altar.* Downers Grove, Ill.: InterVarsity Press, 1985. Subtitled *The Community of Prayer in a Self-Bound Society,* this book places prayer high on the priority list, not only for the individual Christian, but for the corporate church as well. In examining the Psalms, Peterson directs our attention to some of the most moving prayers in all the Scriptures, showing us not only how to nourish our souls, but how to shape society as well.

Tozer, A. W. *The Pursuit of God.* Special edition. Wheaton, Ill.: Tyndale House Publishers, n.d. This book is one of the greatest classics to come from the pen of Dr. A. W. Tozer—pastor, scholar, and Christian statesman. This masterful study of the inner life is not an academic exercise for the mind but an arresting series of sermons that speak to the heart.

White, John. *The Cost of Commitment.* Downers Grove, Ill.: Inter-Varsity Press, 1976. "The Way of the Cross is a magnificent obsession with a heavenly pearl, beside which everything else in life has no value." So writes the author in this compelling discussion on what should be the priority of the church—taking up the cross, not on our lapel or around our necks, but squarely on our shoulders.

IV. Pastor

Hendricks, Howard G. *Teaching to Change Lives.* Portland, Oreg.: Multnomah Press, 1987. This book, written by one of Dallas Theological Seminary's most famous professors, sets out seven laws of teaching that will help you develop a passion for communicating God's Word in your church, home, or Bible study group.

Peterson, Eugene H. *Working the Angles.* Grand Rapids, Mich.: William B. Eerdmans Publishing Co., 1987. In this excellent book, Peterson states that prayer, reading Scripture, and giving spiritual direction are the three basic acts that are critical in determining the shape and scope of a ministry. Only by being attentive to these three acts can pastors fulfill their primary responsibility of keeping the church attentive to God.

White, John. *Excellence in Leadership.* Downers Grove, Ill.: InterVarsity Press, 1986. Subtitled *Reaching Goals with Prayer, Courage and Determination,* this study of Nehemiah provides the model so desperately needed for leaders today.

Acknowledgments

Insight for Living is grateful for permission to quote from the following source:

Tozer, A. W. *God Tells the Man Who Cares.* Harrisburg, Pa.: Christian Publications, 1970.

Notes

Notes

Insight for Living
Cassette Tapes
THE CHURCH: PURPOSE, PROFILE, PRIORITIES

The church has taken a lot of flak over the years, from within her ranks as well as from outside. Unfortunately, the criticism was often justified. The same is true today. Too many of our churches are like ships without sails, pushed aimlessly around by the winds of the world, without purpose or direction.

The whole thrust of this study is that it's time the church got back on course and recovered her sense of responsibility. Through these messages, you'll discover that God's people are not only supposed to make a difference, they're also supposed to *be* different.

			U.S.	Canada
CPP	**CS**	**Cassette series—includes album cover . . . .**	**$29.50**	**$37.50**
		Individual cassettes—include messages A and B	**5.00**	**6.35**

These prices are effective as of May 1988 and are subject to change without notice.

CPP 1-A: ***The Taproot Purpose of Our Existence***
Selected Scripture
B: ***The WIFE Every Church Should Marry***
Acts 2:41–47

CPP 2-A: ***A Closer Look at Our WIFE***
Selected Scripture
B: ***A Church with a Contagious Style***
1 Thessalonians 2:1–13

CPP 3-A: ***Analysis of a Metropolitan Ministry***
Exodus 18:7–24, Ephesians 4:11–16
B: ***Changing Times—Changeless Truths***
Selected Scripture

CPP 4-A: ***Last-Days Lifestyle***
2 Timothy 3:1–4:5
B: ***Stayin' Ready for Quittin' Time***
2 Timothy 3:10–4:5

CPP 5-A: ***The Hardest Part of Harvesting****
Matthew 9:35–38
B: ***No Substitute for Integrity****
National Religious Broadcasters Banquet
Washington, D.C., February 3, 1988

*This message was not a part of the original series but is compatible with it.

How to Order by Mail

Ordering is easy and convenient. Simply mark on the order form whether you want the series or individual tapes, including the quantity you desire. Tear out the order form and mail it with your payment to the appropriate address on the bottom of the form. We will process your order as promptly as we can.

United States orders: If you wish your order to be shipped first-class for faster delivery, please add 10 percent of the total order amount (not including California sales tax). Otherwise, please allow four to six weeks for delivery by fourth-class mail. We accept personal checks, money orders, Visa, and MasterCard in payment for materials. Unfortunately, we are unable to offer invoicing or COD orders.

Canadian orders: Please add 7 percent of your total order for first-class postage and allow approximately four weeks for delivery. For our listeners in British Columbia, a 6 percent sales tax must also be added to the total of all tape orders (not including postage). For further information, please contact our office at 1-800-663-7639. We accept personal checks, money orders, Visa, or MasterCard in payment for materials. Unfortunately, we are unable to offer invoicing or COD orders.

Overseas orders: If you live outside the United States or Canada, please allow six to ten weeks for delivery by surface mail. If you would like your order sent airmail, the delivery time may be reduced. Whether you choose surface or airmail delivery, postage costs must be added to the amount of purchase and included with your order. Please use the following chart to determine the correct postage. Due to fluctuating currency rates, we can accept only personal checks made payable in U.S. funds, international money orders, Visa, or MasterCard in payment for materials.

Type of Postage	Cassettes
Surface	10% of total order
Airmail	25% of total order

For Faster Service, Order by Telephone

To purchase using Visa or MasterCard, you are welcome to use our **toll-free** number between the hours of 8:30 A.M. and 4:00 P.M., Pacific time, Monday through Friday. The number is **1-800-772-8888,** and it may be used anywhere in the United States. Telephone orders from overseas are handled through our Sales Department at (714) 870-9161. Canadian residents should call 1-800-663-7639. We are unable to accept collect calls.

Our Guarantee

Our cassettes are guaranteed for ninety days against faulty performance or breakage due to a defect in the tape. For best results, please be sure your tape recorder is in good operating condition and is cleaned regularly.

Note: To cover processing and handling, there is a $10 fee for *any* returned check.

Order Form

CPP CS represents the entire *The Church: Purpose, Profile, Priorities* series, while CPP 1–5 are the individual tapes included in the series.

Series or Tape	Unit Price U.S.	Unit Price Canada	Quantity	Amount
CPP CS	$29.50	$37.50		$
CPP 1	5.00	6.35		
CPP 2	5.00	6.35		
CPP 3	5.00	6.35		
CPP 4	5.00	6.35		
CPP 5	5.00	6.35		
Subtotal				
Sales tax *6% for orders delivered in California or British Columbia*				
Postage *7% in Canada; overseas residents see "How to Order by Mail"*				
10% optional first-class shipping and handling *U.S. residents only*				
Gift to Insight for Living *Tax-deductible in the U.S. and Canada*				
Total amount due *Please do not send cash.*				$

If there is a balance: ☐ apply it as a donation ☐ please refund

Form of payment:

☐ Check or money order made payable to Insight for Living

☐ Credit card (circle one): Visa MasterCard

Card Number ______________________ Expiration Date ____________

Signature ______________________________________

We cannot process your credit card purchase without your signature.

Name ______________________________________

Address ______________________________________

City ______________________________________

State/Province ______________________ Zip/Postal Code ____________

Country ______________________________________

Telephone (   ) ______________________ Radio Station ___ ___ ___ ___

If questions arise concerning your order, we may need to contact you.

Mail this order form to the Sales Department at one of these addresses:

Insight for Living, Post Office Box 4444, Fullerton, CA 92634

Insight for Living Ministries, Post Office Box 2510, Vancouver, BC, Canada V6B 3W7

Order Form

CPP CS represents the entire *The Church: Purpose, Profile, Priorities* series, while CPP 1–5 are the individual tapes included in the series.

Series or Tape	Unit Price U.S.	Unit Price Canada	Quantity	Amount
CPP CS	$29.50	$37.50		$
CPP 1	5.00	6.35		
CPP 2	5.00	6.35		
CPP 3	5.00	6.35		
CPP 4	5.00	6.35		
CPP 5	5.00	6.35		
			Subtotal	
			Sales tax *6% for orders delivered in California or British Columbia*	
			Postage *7% in Canada; overseas residents see "How to Order by Mail"*	
			10% optional first-class shipping and handling *U.S. residents only*	
			Gift to Insight for Living *Tax-deductible in the U.S. and Canada*	
			Total amount due *Please do not send cash.*	$

If there is a balance: ☐ apply it as a donation ☐ please refund

Form of payment:

☐ Check or money order made payable to Insight for Living

☐ Credit card (circle one): Visa MasterCard

Card Number ______________________ Expiration Date ____________

Signature ______________________________________

We cannot process your credit card purchase without your signature.

Name ______________________________________

Address ______________________________________

City ______________________________________

State/Province ______________________ Zip/Postal Code ____________

Country ______________________________________

Telephone (   ) ______________________ Radio Station ___ ___ ___ ___

If questions arise concerning your order, we may need to contact you.

Mail this order form to the Sales Department at one of these addresses:

Insight for Living, Post Office Box 4444, Fullerton, CA 92634

Insight for Living Ministries, Post Office Box 2510, Vancouver, BC, Canada V6B 3W7

Order Form

CPP CS represents the entire *The Church: Purpose, Profile, Priorities* series, while CPP 1–5 are the individual tapes included in the series.

Series or Tape	Unit Price U.S.	Unit Price Canada	Quantity	Amount
CPP CS	$29.50	$37.50		$
CPP 1	5.00	6.35		
CPP 2	5.00	6.35		
CPP 3	5.00	6.35		
CPP 4	5.00	6.35		
CPP 5	5.00	6.35		
			Subtotal	
			Sales tax *6% for orders delivered in California or British Columbia*	
			Postage *7% in Canada; overseas residents see "How to Order by Mail"*	
			10% optional first-class shipping and handling *U.S. residents only*	
			Gift to Insight for Living *Tax-deductible in the U.S. and Canada*	
			Total amount due *Please do not send cash.*	$

If there is a balance: ☐ apply it as a donation ☐ please refund

Form of payment:

☐ Check or money order made payable to Insight for Living

☐ Credit card (circle one): Visa MasterCard

Card Number ______________________ Expiration Date ____________

Signature ____
We cannot process your credit card purchase without your signature.

Name ____

Address ____

City ____

State/Province ______________________ Zip/Postal Code ____________

Country ____

Telephone (   ) ______________________ Radio Station ____________
If questions arise concerning your order, we may need to contact you.

Mail this order form to the Sales Department at one of these addresses:

Insight for Living, Post Office Box 4444, Fullerton, CA 92634

Insight for Living Ministries, Post Office Box 2510, Vancouver, BC, Canada V6B 3W7